START WATCHING
THE BOOK OF 1 CORINTHIANS
VIDEO BIBLE STUDY

WWW.RIGHTNOWMEDIA.ORG/FIRSTCORINTHIANS

© 2019 by RightNow Ministries

Published by RightNow Ministries
6300 Henneman Way
McKinney, TX 75070
www.rightnow.org

ISBN -978-0-578-42720-1

Printed in the United States of America.

Scripture quotations are from the ESV® Bible (The Holy Bible,
English Standard Version®), copyright © 2001 by Crossway, a
publishing ministry of Good News Publishers. Used by permission. All
rights reserved.

Cover photo © Julia Kaptelova, used with permission.
All other photography © RightNow Ministries.

THE BOOK OF
1ST CORINTHIANS

VIDEO TEACHING FROM JENNIE ALLEN

STUDY GUIDE CURRICULUM BY RIGHTNOW MEDIA

Over the last couple years, our Book of the Bible series has allowed us to visit some amazing places around the world. Sometimes I travel with our RightNow Media team, but I wasn't able to join them on the trip to Greece. So like you, the shots in the video study and the photos in this book help me picture the setting of 1 Corinthians to enhance my reading of the Bible.

As a ministry, our hope is that the videos featuring teaching from Jennie Allen combined with the content of this study guide will deepen your understanding of what God has to say through the book of 1 Corinthians. Jennie is passionate about God's Word and discipleship. I believe you will find her to be a helpful guide on your journey through this book.

Some sections of 1 Corinthians might be familiar, like the "wedding verses" in 1 Corinthians 13, but there's so much more to the letter. This study is an opportunity to take a closer look at what God teaches us through the apostle Paul's writings. I pray God speaks to you through this study.

The mission of the church matters!

Brian Mosley
President, RightNow Ministries

HOW TO USE THIS STUDY GUIDE

Welcome to RightNow Media's *The Book of 1 Corinthians Study Guide*. What you hold in your hands is meant to be more than an intellectual analysis of Paul's letter. It's a journey intended to lead you through his words to the fledgling church in Corinth. This guide will require more of you than simply reading the Bible and answering a few questions. It'll ask you to engage your heart and your hands as well—feeling the full impact of Paul's writing as well as putting into action the challenges his letter makes to his readers.

This guide is broken out into twelve weeks, each one corresponding to RightNow Media's video Bible study series, *The Book of 1 Corinthians*, featuring Jennie Allen. Each week features an introduction and small group questions you can use to discuss the video and Bible passage in a group setting. There are five days' worth of devotional activities per week that will both dig into the text of the letter as well as offer opportunities to put into practice the life-changing truths in Paul's words. It's up to you how you break up the days across your week. The first day of each week focuses specifically on Jennie's teaching, and the rest offers deeper study of the text.

Each week begins with three goals: life-change in your mind, your emotions, and your actions. Everything that follows in the week aims at helping you practically apply the truths in Paul's letter to your life in order to achieve those goals.

Throughout the guide, you'll find bolded questions or action points that ask you to do something with what you're studying. There's also space in the guide to write down notes, prayers, or answers to questions.

You'll find a small number corresponding to the question in that space, which should help you keep track of what item your writing corresponds to. You're definitely not limited to that space, however. This book is just a guide.

As you work through the book, you'll find more than just the words on the page. Jennie's teaching in each video session will set up the week for you and help orient you to that week's passage. You'll also encounter deeper looks at the original language in Paul's letter as well as other helpful explanations of sticky issues.

If you're using this book as part of a group study, consider watching the video teaching together and discussing the questions listed in the book. Then, throughout the week, work through the remaining five days of questions. When you get together again, talk through your week's study before moving on to the next session.

In the end, this book is a guide on a journey through 1 Corinthians. Paul's letter challenges the Corinthians to take a risk—to put other people before themselves. The guide you hold in your hands, along with the teaching from Jennie Allen, will lead you through 1 Corinthians. At the end of the journey—and at the end of this book—you'll have a very important question to answer: Will you take the risk?

WEEKLY GOALS

Each week begins with three life change goals aimed at your mind, emotions, and actions.

Reject Cultural Norms

VIDEO SESSIONS

Begin each week by watching the corresponding video session.

"
When you live differently, the world won't like it.
"

DISCUSSION QUESTIONS

These questions are for small group discussion on Jennie's teaching and the passage from 1 Corinthians.

Day One

ACTION POINTS

Each day's questions and challenges are marked with small numbers to help you stay organized.

JOURNAL SECTION

There's space in the guide to write down notes, prayers, or answers to questions.

Know The Problem

SESSION ONE

Welcome to the book of 1 Corinthians. As we study this letter, we'll step into ancient Corinth while reading the words Paul wrote to the fledgling church. We're going to see that, like all churches, the Corinthian church wasn't perfect. They had a problem. A big problem. And it grew to such an epic proportion that it poisoned the church in various ways. Paul wrote to provide the antidote.

In this study, we're going to explore Paul's solution to both the problems in Corinth and in us. Through his words, we'll learn more about Jesus's plan for a people who live radically different lives than the world around them. But we'll also take a hard look in the mirror and ask the Spirit to point out our own self-centered attitudes.

Reading the Bible isn't just something we do to impress people or to check off on a to-do list. It's about getting to know God. It's about shaping every minute of our lives to reflect Jesus. It's about thinking differently in the power of the Spirit.

So as we approach each week, we'll focus on one main idea. That main idea will point us to change how we think, feel, and act.

This week, we'll see that resolving relational disunity begins in our hearts, because division is a symptom of self-focus. From this main idea, we have three goals:

- We want to understand that selfishness has dire consequences, both in the local church and in us as individuals.

- We want to feel motivated to reject selfishness and embrace a life that's Christ-and-others-centered.

- We want to identify and turn away from the ways we're holding on to selfishness.

Keep the main idea in your mind as we go through the first chapter of 1 Corinthians this week.

WATCH SESSION 1

THE BOOK OF 1 CORINTHIANS

WITH JENNIE ALLEN

These questions come from the free Facilitator's Guide for *The Book of 1 Corinthians* on RightNow Media's website. If you're leading a group, download the Facilitator's Guide to help lead discussion on Jennie's teaching and the passage from 1 Corinthians.

1   AFTER READING THE INTRODUCTORY VERSES AND LISTENING TO JENNIE, WHAT'S YOUR IMPRESSION OF THE CHURCH IN CORINTH? WHAT'S WRONG WITH THE CHURCH?

2   BASED OFF CHAPTER 1 AND JENNIE'S TEACHING, IN WHAT WAYS ARE THE CORINTHIANS BEING SELFISH?

3   LOOKING AT YOUR OWN LIFE, WHERE DO YOU FEEL THE STRUGGLE BETWEEN WANTING TO DO THINGS YOUR WAY VERSUS JESUS'S WAY? WHICH ONE USUALLY WINS?

4   JENNIE TALKED ABOUT HOW PAUL DEPENDED ON THE SPIRIT. WHAT DOES IT LOOK LIKE FOR SOMEONE TO RELY ON THE SPIRIT? WHAT'S DIFFERENT ABOUT THAT PERSON?

5   WHAT'S ONE THING YOU COULD DO THIS WEEK TO BE SELFLESS TOWARD ANOTHER PERSON?

"

This book is not just for Corinth—it's also for us.

"

Day One

First Corinthians will take us on a journey. We'll look at the struggles of one of the first local churches in all of history. We'll see that the Corinthians weren't much different from us. And we'll realize that Paul's words to them still ring true today.

[1] **But before we jump into 1 Corinthians, spend a few minutes writing out a short prayer to God. Ask him to use this study to change you.**

Open up your Bible to 1 Corinthians. Go ahead and read the entire first chapter. As you read, ask yourself this question: What was the problem in the Corinthian church?

Take a look at verses 10 and 11. The Corinthian church suffered from division. We'll see it all throughout the book. The struggling church fought over leadership, spiritual gifts, food, marriage, and theology. Since the theme of disunity runs throughout the letter, it's tempting to think that was the church's problem.

But it wasn't. Disunity was only a symptom of a far more insidious—and common— disease.

Jennie pointed out the real issue that was going on in Corinth. Did you catch it? She said they were selfish. They were so consumed with themselves that they tried to solve their problems their own way, held on to their culture, and, as a result, blasted chasms between them and other Christians.

No one likes to admit to selfishness—especially people who claim to follow Jesus. But it often sneaks into our lives in ways we don't readily see. And then it spills over in ways we never expect. For the Corinthians, their selfishness led to severe divisions in the church. What is it for us? We'll spend the rest of the study unpacking that very question.

² **Now that we know the main problem Paul's tackling in 1 Corinthians, take a moment to be honest with God. Write down any fears or concerns you have about confronting the problem of selfishness. Ask God to use this study to turn your gaze to him.**

¹⁰ *I appeal to you, brothers, by the name of our Lord Jesus Christ, that all of you agree, and that there be no divisions among you, but that you be united in the same mind and the same judgment. ¹¹ For it has been reported to me by Chloe's people that there is quarreling among you, my brothers.*

1 CORINTHIANS 1:10−11

Day Two

Before we dive further into 1 Corinthians, let's pause and get our bearings. Letters are always written to a specific person or people in a certain time and setting. In order to best understand a letter, we have to know its author, audience, and occasion.

AUTHOR AND OCCASION

Paul the apostle wrote 1 Corinthians to a church he planted during his second missionary journey. You can read Acts 18:1–17 to learn more about Paul's experience in Corinth.

Paul left the church after a year and a half of ministry. Before writing 1 Corinthians, Paul had written another letter to the church to address some other issues. Paul references that letter in 1 Corinthians because the people didn't listen the first time.

Flip over to 1 Corinthians 1:11. While in Ephesus on his third missionary journey, Paul heard that the church in Corinth wasn't doing well. He also received a letter from the Corinthians with questions for him. Paul decided it was time to write the Corinthian church to speak to the issues they brought up and the ones reported to him by other church members.

AREOPAGUS (MARS HILL)
The Areopagus, also known as "Mars Hill," is a rocky hill that overlooks Athens. During biblical times, it was a common meeting place for debating the philosophies of the day. It's also where Paul shared the gospel by appealing to the Athenians' "unknown god" in Acts 17:16–34.

AUDIENCE

Corinth was one of the richest city-states in the Roman Empire. The city had temples to many gods, the most prominent being the temple to Aphrodite, which was known for its prostitutes.

Paul wrote to people who lived much different lives than we do today—and yet they weren't that much different from us in a lot of ways. Corinth was a place of wealth, sex, and power. And, as we'll see throughout 1 Corinthians, the church let the culture influence it in more ways than one.

Now, it's important to note that culture isn't always bad. Sometimes it can be a source of good. But in the case of the Corinthians, they selfishly held onto the godless pieces of their culture, wealth, and status to such a degree that it caused division in the church.

To finish off today's session, take a few minutes to think about the culture you live in and the way it affects you. Look around you. In what ways are you a product of your culture? What've you come to rely on in your culture? What would be difficult to give up to follow Jesus?

We'll see throughout this study that the Christian life is not without sacrifice—giving up the things that keep us self-focused instead of Jesus-and-others-focused. Sacrifice is the hardest part of following Jesus, and it starts with recognizing what we're afraid to give up.

Day Three

So far this week, we've looked at the big problem in the Corinthian church and we've learned some more about Paul and the city of Corinth. Let's take a deeper look at the actual letter. Read 1 Corinthians 1:1–9. As you read, notice how many times Paul mentions Jesus.

Paul starts off by reminding the Corinthians of the salvation they've received through Jesus. He doesn't want them to forget it. Beginning in verse 4, he lists off all the ways the Corinthians have received God's generosity. **Go back through verses 4–9. Write down anything that the Corinthians have received as a result of God's grace.**

Take a look at your list. It's true Paul wrote to a specific church in a certain situation. But what's amazing is that God's kindness to the Corinthians is true for you too. If you're a follower of Jesus, you've also received God's grace.

But what exactly is grace? We talk about it all the time in church circles. Do we know what it actually means?

THE BOOK OF 1ST CORINTHIANS

Think of it this way. Imagine you're in a car accident—and it's entirely your fault. Instead of an angry driver demanding your insurance information, picture the person you hit writing you a check in the amount it would cost you to buy a brand new Ferrari.

It doesn't make sense. It's extravagant. In the eyes of the world, it's wasteful at best and simply stupid at worst.

An undeserved car doesn't even begin to illustrate the sacrificial love God has shown us through Jesus. Look at the list you wrote earlier. None of us deserves any of those things. But God has given them to those who believe in him anyway. He's written us the most outlandish check.

That's why Paul mentions Jesus nine times in just nine verses. And it's why Paul always talks about Jesus combined with the word, "Christ." The word "Christ" is the Greek translation of the Hebrew word "Messiah," who was the anticipated savior of Israel.

So when Paul writes "Christ," he's alluding to Jesus's ministry—his death and resurrection and the salvation that comes through him. It's everything Jesus, the Messiah, did. Jesus—all that he's done and all of who he is—is evidence of God's grace in our lives.

Paul wants the Corinthians to remember the true source of everything good they experience in life and every hope they have for life after death.

That's true for the Corinthians. And it's true for us.

End your time today by writing out a prayer of thanks to God—look at the prayer Paul wrote in verses 4–9 if you need inspiration. Thank God for his grace in your life. Thank him for Jesus.

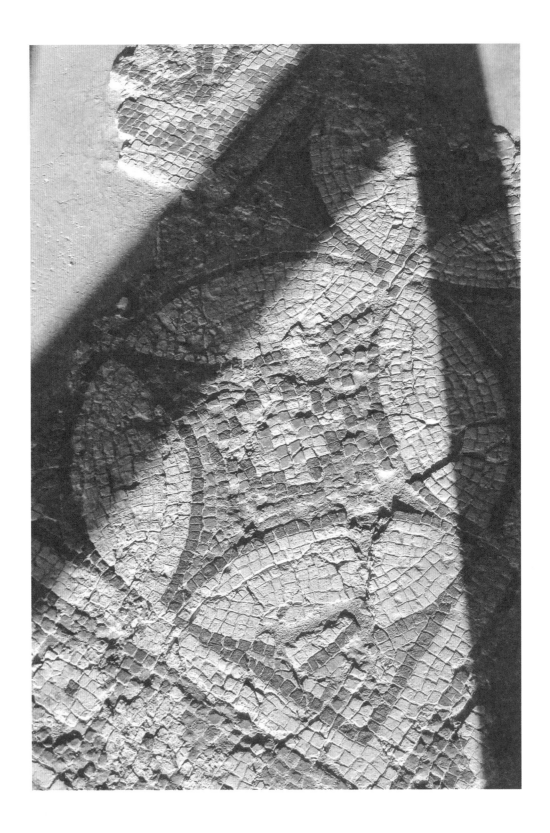

Day Four

Yesterday, we talked about the grace we've been given through Jesus. We have our "ticket" to heaven. We have a new life in this world. The rest should be simple, right?

No matter how long you've been following Jesus, you know that isn't true. The Christian life is more than just a one-time decision to give your life to Jesus. It's also a thousand little decisions to continually choose Jesus over self. And sometimes we feel the tension between Jesus's way of living and the way we want to live.

The Corinthians felt that tension too. Read 1 Corinthians 1:10–17. **What were the Corinthians doing that caused division in their local church?**

The church members are latched onto different leaders—Paul, Apollos, Cephas (or Peter), and Jesus. They're playing a church version of "My dad's stronger than your dad." It's causing division and Paul's not happy about it.

Paul's adamant throughout this section that no church is about him or other teachers. It's about Jesus and his gospel. In verse 17, he goes as far to say that eloquent teaching—whether from him or anyone else—zaps the power from the cross of Christ.

Why do you think something like eloquent teaching or who-baptized-whom takes away the power of the cross of Jesus? What are people concerned about when they focus on those things?

It all comes back to what we talked about on day one—selfishness. The Corinthians chose prestige, power, and authority over Jesus. That's why they're bragging about certain leaders. And that's why there's division. In the tense fight of allegiance, the Corinthians have allowed selfishness to win.

Looking at your own life, where do you feel the struggle between wanting to do things your way versus Jesus's way? Which one usually wins?

The bottom line for the Corinthians—and for us—comes down to a simple question: Will you let go? We face the same temptation the Corinthians did—to hold on to security and pleasure and comfort as if our lives depended on it. To let selfishness win.

Take a look at verse 17. Paul understood what it meant to let go. As Jennie pointed out, his life wasn't centered on himself but on Christ and the church instead. That's the life we should be after.

So the question is, will you let go?

Day Five

People in Paul's day highly valued wisdom. People would gather in public places to hear each other's arguments and debate new ideas. Those with the tightest arguments and best delivery were revered. Jennie spoke about a time when Paul attempted to reason with the people of Athens in Acts 17:16–34.

We know from 1 Corinthians 1:17 that Paul wasn't about impressing people with his words. His only concern was the gospel. But, as we've seen this week, the people of Corinth were heavily influenced by their culture's definition of eloquence and wisdom. So Paul continues his argument to show them that the things the world values pale in comparison to God.

Read 1 Corinthians 1:18–31. While you're reading, notice how many times Paul mentions wisdom, foolishness, and power.

¹⁸ For the word of the cross is folly to those who are perishing, but to us who are being saved it is the power of God. ¹⁹ For it is written,

"I will destroy the wisdom of the wise, and the discernment of the discerning I will thwart."

²⁰ Where is the one who is wise? Where is the scribe? Where is the debater of this age? Has not God made foolish the wisdom of the world? ²¹ For since, in the wisdom of God, the world did not know God through wisdom, it pleased God through the folly of what we preach to save those who believe. ²² For Jews demand signs and Greeks seek wisdom, ²³ but we preach Christ crucified, a stumbling block to Jews and folly to Gentiles, ²⁴ but to those who are called, both Jews and Greeks, Christ the power of God and the wisdom of God. ²⁵ For the foolishness of God is wiser than men, and the weakness of God is stronger than men.

²⁶ For consider your calling, brothers: not many of you were wise according to worldly standards, not many were powerful, not many were of noble birth. ²⁷ But God chose what is foolish in the world to shame the wise; God chose what is weak in the world to shame the strong; ²⁸ God chose what is low and despised in the world, even things that are not, to bring to nothing things that are, ²⁹ so that no human being might boast in the presence of God. ³⁰ And because of him you are in Christ Jesus, who became to us wisdom from God, righteousness and sanctification and redemption, ³¹ so that, as it is written, "Let the one who boasts, boast in the Lord."

1 CORINTHIANS 1:18–31

After reading the passage, how would you define the world's wisdom? What about God's?

Paul sets up God's wisdom and the world's wisdom as opposing each other. God's ways often look like folly to the world, but in the end it's actually the world that's got it wrong. The fact that the Corinthians are putting all their chips on certain leaders falls into the category of worldly wisdom—it's actually foolish.

But then Paul turns the tables on the Corinthians. He tells them that they were foolish, weak, and despised even before Christ. They've got nothing to show for their salvation. But, even so, God chose them. And he chose you.

Think about it. You had nothing to offer God. Nothing. But he chose to save you. To give you life. To bring you into his family. That's good news.

Spend a few minutes journaling about the fact that you came to God with nothing, but he gave you everything. How does that truth sit with you? How has it changed the way you think? The way you live?

In 1 Corinthians 1:30–31, Paul brings us back to the main idea we talked about in day one. We can choose selfishness and boast in ourselves, the leader we follow, or the person who baptized us. Or we can choose the selfless way—the way that often looks foolish to the world—and boast in God.

Which will you choose?

Follow The Spirit

Last week, we asked the question, "Will you let go?" It's a question we all have to answer as Christians. Will we hold on to our comfort, security, and safety? Or will we risk it all by putting Jesus—and everyone else—first?

This week we're going to look at *why* we should let go. We talk a lot about why following Jesus is worth it. But sometimes we only talk about the things that will someday come—eternity with him, resurrection, innocence on judgment day. But what kind of difference does it make in our lives today?

So far in 1 Corinthians, Paul has been setting up two ways of going about the Christian life. The Corinthians were trying to be just like the world while also trying to be Christians. Their eyes turned inward. Their immaturity caused division in the church. Paul proposes a different way—a risk-filled life of choosing to look foolish, of putting other people before yourself, of letting go of cultural comforts.

This week, we're going to look at the difference between the worldly way of approaching the Christian life and the way Paul describes. Choosing the "risky" life led by the Spirit might look crazy to the world, but it's worth it because we're never alone and we're free from judgment from other people.

Through this week's study, we want to:

• Know why choosing the risk of a life led by the Spirit is worth it.

• Feel freedom from other people's judgment and the worries we face.

• Take active steps toward letting go of any person, habit, or thing that keeps us from risking a selfless life.

Keep those things in mind as we go through this week's study.

WATCH SESSION 2
THE BOOK OF 1 CORINTHIANS
WITH JENNIE ALLEN

These questions come from the free Facilitator's Guide for *The Book of 1 Corinthians* on
RightNow Media's website. If you're leading a group, download the Facilitator's Guide
to help lead discussion on Jennie's teaching and the passage from 1 Corinthians.

1   WHAT PROBLEM DOES PAUL ADDRESS IN THIS SECTION OF 1 CORINTHIANS?
    WHAT WERE THE CHRISTIANS IN CORINTH FIGHTING ABOUT?

2   JENNIE SAID, "WE TEND TO WORSHIP PEOPLE INSTEAD OF GOD." WHAT DOES THAT MEAN?
    WHEN DO YOU FEEL THE TEMPTATION TO WORSHIP PEOPLE INSTEAD OF GOD?

3   JENNIE DESCRIBED TWO WAYS OF LIVING: THE WORLD'S WAY OR GOD'S WAY. HOW WOULD YOU DESCRIBE
    THE DIFFERENCE BETWEEN THESE TWO WAYS OF LIVING? WHICH ONE IS MORE DIFFICULT TO FOLLOW?
    WHAT MAKES IT DIFFICULT?

4   DESCRIBE A TIME WHEN FOLLOWING THE SPIRIT FELT "FOOLISH" TO YOU. WHAT DID YOU DO?
    WHAT WAS THE RESULT?

5   WHAT'S ONE AREA OF YOUR LIFE WHERE YOU SEE YOURSELF LEANING AWAY FROM THE SPIRIT'S LEADING?
    WHAT COULD YOU DO THIS WEEK TO TRUST HIM WITH THAT AREA OF YOUR LIFE?

"

There's a way to live that's wholly other, set apart.

"

Day One

Have you ever looked like a complete fool? Maybe you've spilled coffee on your lap before a meeting or you've had a laughing fit in the middle of a serious movie. We've all been there. We've all done something embarrassing—something against the societal norm.

We've already talked about the risk of the selfless life Paul advocates in 1 Corinthians. Jennie continued to explain the difference between living for yourself—the way the world lives—and living for Christ and his church. She said the living-for-others life looks absolutely foolish to the world.

Take a few minutes to write about what could make choosing the risky, Jesus-and-others-centered life feel foolish. Maybe it could mean stopping a complete stranger to pray for them or giving away your paycheck to a family in need. Why do you think those things might feel foolish? How might other people react?

Space to write on the next page... 39

As Jennie described, the life we've been called into—and the life Paul's talking about in this section of 1 Corinthians—looks backwards to outsiders. But we're going to see through this section of Paul's letter that it's worth choosing.

Carve out some time to read through 1 Corinthians 2 and 3 today. As you read, look for evidence that the Corinthians had chosen the familiar path paved by the world.

The Corinthians had chosen Christ but they were trying to live the Christian life on their own terms. Instead of operating in the power of the Spirit, they held on to the way they lived before Paul showed up in Corinth with the gospel.

The Corinthian version of Christianity was safe. Their lives looked like everyone else's, with a little bit of Jesus sprinkled here and there. Paul pits their way of life against his own to show how choosing the foolish way instead of the easy way is worth it.

Before we go any further, pause and reflect on your life as a Christian. When have you been more like the Corinthians who believed in Jesus but lived like everyone else? Or when have you lived the upside-down life Paul talks about? Where do you see yourself now? Spend a few minutes praying through your answers to these questions. Thank God for journey he's taken you on so far and pray for continued growth with him moving forward.

Whether you feel more like Paul or the Corinthians, we're going to keep asking the same question we posed in session one: Will you let go? Will you let go of the safe, familiar life? Will you choose the risky life?

It's up to you to answer.

Day Two

Some of us love to speak in front of people, while some of us would rather eat a bucket of sardines. In this section of 1 Corinthians 2, we're going to look at a time in Paul's past where he spoke publicly to the smartest people of his day . . . and completely failed.

Open your Bible to 1 Corinthians 2 and read verses 1–5. While you're reading, think back to Jennie's teaching in the last session about Acts 17, where Paul used his wisdom and wit to debate people in Athens. If you're having trouble remembering the story, go ahead and read Acts 17:16–34. **¹How might Paul's experience at Athens prompt him to write these words in chapter 2 to the Corinthians?**

Paul's speech in Athens didn't go well. A few people believed, but most mocked him and went on their way. Right after his failure to persuade the Athenian intellectual elite, Paul went to Corinth. He spends verses 1–5 of chapter 2 describing how he preached the gospel to the Corinthians.

²What's the difference between how Paul preached to the Corinthians versus the Athenians?

Paul came to Corinth weak. He had given his best effort at formulating a persuasive argument in Athens and it didn't go as well as he had hoped. When he showed up in Corinth, he was afraid and worn out. He chose to preach only about Jesus being a self-sacrificing savior—a message that sounded crazy to the self-centered Corinthians.

The difference? Paul made the unglamorous choice to depend on the Spirit. To focus on others. The result? The Spirit spoke. The Corinthians believed.

For Paul, debating and speech-giving would have felt normal. He used to be a Pharisee, which meant he'd spend hours debating the Old Testament with other Pharisees. Choosing to form an eloquent argument would have been self-reliant and safe. What he did in Corinth was risky, terrifying, and ultimately selfless.

Describe a time when you felt God asking you to do something that terrified you. Why were you afraid? What did you end up doing?

This passage reminds us that fear doesn't necessarily go away when we choose the foolish-to-the-world way of the Spirit. Paul was afraid, and rightly so. This passage also begins to show us why it's worth it to choose to let go. When Paul let go of what he could do himself, the Spirit took over and the Corinthians believed the gospel.

Paul let go of his eloquence and earthly wisdom. He let go of the desire to sound smart to the people he spoke to. He let go of his past failure.

What about you? Take some time to talk with God. Just you and him. Ask him what you need to let go of. Maybe it's something from your past. Maybe it's how you manage your money. Maybe it's your fixation on what people think about you. Hold those things in your mind as we move through this week.

Day Three

We want the things we do and the choices we make to be worth it. The same goes for living the Christian life. Is it worth it to risk living this scary, foolish life Paul's been talking about?

Open your Bible up to 1 Corinthians 2 and read verses 6–16.

Paul's back to contrasting the wisdom of the world with God's wisdom just like he did in chapter 1. Except this time, he's putting a magnifying lens up to the wisdom of God so we can see what it means to have God's wisdom through the Spirit in us.

Take a look at verses 10–13. Paul highlights several things the Spirit does for us. He gives us access to the mind of God. He helps us speak with the wisdom of God. But most importantly, he is *with* us.

Did you catch that? He's with you. No matter what.

PARTHENON
Constructed in 5th century B.C., the Parthenon was the most prominent temple dedicated to the goddess Athena in the city of Athens. Commonly associated with wisdom and warfare, the temple demonstrates the love of many gods and ideas in Athens, also a hallmark of Corinthian culture.

Whether you feel alone in a crowd or are having the best day ever, God is with you. When you lose your job or buy a house or switch churches, he's there. You're never alone.

Spend a few minutes reflecting on a time when you were aware of the Spirit's presence with you. What was going on at the time? What did the Spirit do to remind you that he was there?

The benefits of having the Spirit don't stop there. Read verse 15 again. When we tap into the power of the Spirit—when we give into the risky Christian life—the Spirit does the work. If people judge us for what we do or say, their judgment isn't directed at us. It's directed at the Spirit.

When have you felt judged for choosing to be others-focused? What difference does it make to know that the judgment you faced was actually directed at the Spirit?

Choosing the backwards-to-the-world way of the Spirit is worth it. We have the Spirit of God with us and he does the work. We're free from judgment from people. We aren't alone.

While the Christian life isn't about what we get, it's nice to know that choosing it is worth putting our own self-interests at risk.

So as you go about your day today, pick something that's part of your routine—maybe getting into your car, or eating a meal, or brushing your teeth—and use that time to pause and remember that the Spirit of God is with you. Say a short prayer to thank God for all the Spirit gives you—his presence, freedom from judgment, and wisdom.

Day Four

We've all given the Bible a double take. Maybe for you it was when you were breezing through a gospel and had to stop and re-read a section a few times wondering, "Did Jesus really say that?" Or maybe you had to scan back through a passage in Leviticus because it made no sense to you.

The Bible has sticky sections. And, while it's tempting to skim over those passages, it's better for us in the long run to wrestle with the difficult questions instead of brushing them aside.

We're going to see that 1 Corinthians has a lot of sticky sections. Sometimes we'll pause from our study to investigate what they mean, and sometimes not. Today we're going to look at two parts of chapter 3 that we often misunderstand or don't understand at all. Grab your Bible and open up to 1 Corinthians 3. Read verses 10–17.

---

[10] According to the grace of God given to me, like a skilled master builder I laid a foundation, and someone else is building upon it. Let each one take care how he builds upon it. [11] For no one can lay a foundation other than that which is laid, which is Jesus Christ. [12] Now if anyone builds on the foundation with gold, silver, precious stones, wood, hay, straw— [13] each one's work will become manifest, for the Day will disclose it, because it will be revealed by fire, and the fire will test what sort of work each one has done. [14] If the work that anyone has built on the foundation survives, he will receive a reward. [15] If anyone's work is burned up, he will suffer loss, though he himself will be saved, but only as through fire.

[16] Do you not know that you are God's temple and that God's Spirit dwells in you? [17] If anyone destroys God's temple, God will destroy him. For God's temple is holy, and you are that temple.

1 CORINTHIANS 3:10–17

As you read, answer the following questions:

What specific kind of "work" is Paul talking about in verses 12–15?

Who's Paul talking about in verses 16–17?

Now, a lot of times we read verses 12–15 as applying to every believer and start freaking out. Will we barely make it through the fire? But that's not really what Paul's getting at.

He's focused on church leaders—those who help God's people grow. In verses 5–9, Paul explains that, while church leaders play an important role, God's the one who brings the growth to the church.

So if you're a leader in your church, take this passage seriously. But if not, don't stress about what will or won't make it through the fire. That's not your concern.

That brings us to the next set of verses. We often read verses 16–17 as being about us as individuals. But they aren't. The Greek pronouns in these verses are plural, meaning Paul's talking about all Christians. We, collectively, make up God's temple. What Paul's saying here is a big deal. God's presence isn't confined to a single place or a single person. He's with all of us—all of his people. We're a part of something bigger than ourselves.

So how should that truth change how we live? **Spend some time thinking about your local church. How likely are you to sacrifice time to serve people from your church?**

And then take a moment to think about your day. What could you do to remind someone in your church that they're not alone—maybe through a phone call, a meal, or a note?

Day Five

We all have times in our lives when we were less mature than we are now. Just think back to middle school and it'll probably prove the point. We all have to grow up sometime. We can't act like we're in kindergarten if we're actually an adult.

The same goes for how we grow as Christians. We should move past how we acted, thought, and spoke when we first started following Jesus.

Spend a few minutes writing about when you first believed in Jesus. What kinds of things have changed in the way you live since then? Who has set an example for you of how to think about other people? Where do you see room to improve in the way you treat others?

The problem comes when we stay put—when we don't grow up as Christians. That's part of the Corinthians' problem and Paul calls them out on it. **Read 1 Corinthians 3:1–23. While you're reading, jot down the signs that point to the Corinthians' immaturity.**

The Corinthians wanted both the Christian life and the worldly life everyone else had in the city. Remember that, at that time, people lifted wisdom—particularly wise leaders—onto a pedestal. The Corinthians arguing about which leader they follow would have been the cultural norm in Corinth.

So, in this section, Paul attacks their need to rally behind, rely on, and brag about certain leaders.

Paul has harsh words for the Corinthians. He calls them childish and worldly. They're too immature to recognize God's role in their growth. And they're too arrogant to see that what they're doing goes against the life God's called them to. They've mistaken God's work for human work. They've idolized human leaders over God.

And we can do the same. We can look at how our lives have unfolded and forget God's role in all of it. When we neglect to remember that God's in the middle of it all with us, we worry.

Sometimes when we're worried, our immediate reaction is to go looking for comfort. For some people that could be alcohol, shopping, social media, video games, or a TV show. But if we think that's the best way to live the Christian life, we're just like the Corinthians. We're deceiving ourselves.

Pause for a few minutes to be honest before God. Confess any ways you might be turning to something—or someone—else besides God with your worries. Tell him what you're worried about. Ask him for opportunities to go to him with your worries this week.

When we allow God to dig up the deep-rooted ways we resist the selfless life God's called us into, we grow. Or rather, he grows us. Let's praise him for that.

Reject Cultural Norms

SESSION THREE

So far in our study of 1 Corinthians, we've been taking a hard look at the risk of the others-centered life Jesus calls us into. We've seen the selfish route of the Corinthians who held on to the world while also trying to follow Christ. We've looked at the benefits of choosing to focus all our attention and efforts outside of ourselves.

In this week's trek through 1 Corinthians 4, we're going to learn how counter-cultural the "foolish" life of Jesus and his followers really is.

We've already touched on this truth a little bit in the series. Paul's pointed out the surface issues where the Corinthians are trying to be like the world: their approach to wisdom and charismatic leaders.

But in this chapter, Paul takes it a step further. He speaks against what's assumed in the culture—the things that are so ingrained people hardly notice they're there. He pushes against consumerism, celebrity, and self-centered power.

And we'll also see how each of those things is still an issue in the church today.

By taking a deeper look at the counter-cultural Christian life, we want to:

• Recognize the ways we've integrated self-centered cultural norms into our lives and attitudes toward our local church.

• Feel conviction over the ways we're holding on to what the world says we should do rather than what Christ says.

• Reject the cultural norms we've latched on to by giving them up and choosing to focus our attention and energy on God and others.

Keep those things in mind as we go through this week's passage.

These questions come from the free Facilitator's Guide for *The Book of 1 Corinthians* on
RightNow Media's website. If you're leading a group, download the Facilitator's Guide
to help lead discussion on Jennie's teaching and the passage from 1 Corinthians.

1   IN WHAT WAYS HAD THE CORINTHIANS BOUGHT INTO THE CULTURAL NORMS OF THE DAY?
    WERE THOSE NORMS GODLY? WHY NOT?

2   WHAT ARE SOME EXAMPLES OF GODLESS CULTURAL NORMS THAT HAVE SEEPED INTO THE CHURCH?
    HOW HAVE THEY AFFECTED YOUR ATTITUDE TOWARD CHURCH, OTHER CHRISTIANS, OR YOURSELF?

3   WHAT DIFFERENCE DOES IT MAKE TO YOU TO KNOW THAT YOU BELONG TO CHRIST AND NOT YOURSELF?
    IN WHAT WAYS DOES THAT IDEA PUSH AGAINST THE MESSAGE THE CULTURE SAYS ABOUT YOU?

4   WHAT FEARS OR CONCERNS DO YOU HAVE ABOUT GOING AGAINST THE CULTURAL NORM
    IN FAVOR OF GODLINESS?

5   THINK OF ONE CULTURAL NORM THAT AFFECTS YOU EVERY DAY. WHAT COULD IT LOOK LIKE FOR YOU
    TO GO AGAINST THAT NORM IN YOUR SCHOOL, WORK, OR HOME THIS WEEK?

"

When you live differently, the world won't like it.

"

Day One

For the past two weeks, we've unpacked Paul's frustrations with the Corinthians. They're selfish. They've adopted a Jesus-plus-the-world attitude toward the Christian life. It's played out in how they're using church leaders to fight with each other.

Grab your Bible and open up to 1 Corinthians 4. We're not going to do an extensive study of the chapter today. We're just going to read it for now.

As you read, can you feel Paul's frustration in the passage? He's fed up with how the Corinthians are living. They're bragging about their favorite leaders. They're acting like they're wiser than everyone else. They're causing division.

Chapter 4 wraps up Paul's argument against the Corinthians' behavior toward their leaders. This week, we're going to see how Paul's words speak to some of the deepest issues in the Corinthian church and how those same issues also exist in us.

Jennie talked in the video about what it means to truly live the life Jesus has called us to. It's completely counter-cultural. It's risky. It's in tension with the life the world tells us to lead. Things like consumerism, celebrity, and self-centered power contradict the Jesus-and-others-centered way of living.

Jennie challenged us to be counter-cultural, but to do so while remembering God's love. This week is going to be a tough one. Paul isn't messing around—he's calling out some serious issues in the church. We're going to talk about each of them. But before we do, let's begin by remembering the most important thing about us.

God loves us. He loves you.

Any rebuke, correction, or discipline from God about the way we're living comes from someone who deeply loves us.

That will never change.

Spend the next five minutes reminding yourself that God loves you by identifying a moment in your life when you knew beyond the shadow of a doubt that God loved you. Sit with God for a while and thank him for loving you.

Hold on to those memories as well as the gospel story this week.

And remember that you are loved.

★ ODEON OF HERODUS ATTICUS
This ancient theater for music was built to seat nearly five thousand people. Its placement on the Acropolis, the central hub of ancient Athens, shows the importance of consumer entertainment to the people of its day.

Day Two

In the video, Jennie reminded us that we live in a consumeristic world. All you have to do is take a drive down a major road to know it's true. Billboards and ads tell us we need more—more food, more pleasure, more gadgets—and that we should do whatever it takes to get it.

Take a few minutes to journal about how our culture of consumerism might be affecting your relationship with God. What do you hope to get from him? If he never gave you what you wanted, would you still follow him?

Space to write on the next page... 67

The people in Corinth also lived in a consumeristic culture. They were used to comfortable lives filled with luxury imports, temple prostitutes, and live entertainment. While the specifics of their consumerism might be different than ours, the sentiment is the same. They wanted more. Whatever the cost.

Re-read 1 Corinthians 4:8. As we've seen before in this letter, the Corinthians were living however they wanted. Paul calls them "kings." In contrast with the lives of the apostles—who were beaten, imprisoned, and mocked—the Corinthians had little to complain about. But instead of living for Jesus, they were fighting over which leader gave the best sermons.

It's uncomfortable to admit, but we're a lot like the Corinthians. We can make Sunday morning about our worship preference or favorite sermon style. The celebrity culture that's trickled into Christian circles can distract us too.

But Jesus didn't come, die, and rise from the dead so we could treat him—and the people who follow him—like a Netflix queue. We can't pick and choose the parts of Christianity that we like, discard what we don't, and set some things aside for later.

Following Jesus is an all-or-nothing kind of life.

The consumerism mindset doesn't stop with how we live the Christian life. It trickles into what we think about Jesus too. **Let that truth sit with you for a few minutes. What do you expect from Jesus? Are you more interested in following him or in what he can give you?**

¹⁴ I do not write these things to make you ashamed, but to admonish you as my beloved children. ¹⁵ For though you have countless guides in Christ, you do not have many fathers. For I became your father in Christ Jesus through the gospel. ¹⁶ I urge you, then, be imitators of me. ¹⁷ That is why I sent you Timothy, my beloved and faithful child in the Lord, to remind you of my ways in Christ, as I teach them everywhere in every church.

1 CORINTHIANS 4:14–17

Day Three

Yesterday was tough. We had to look a huge aspect of our culture—consumerism—in the eye and see how it affects our churches and us. It plays out in our attitude toward leaders, Sunday morning services, and each other.

Paul's been pushing against the Corinthians' consumeristic mindset. He's adamant that the Corinthians shouldn't use Christian leaders as a leg up or a spiritual crutch.

But it begs the question, what *should* we expect from the Christian celebrities and leaders in our lives? What should our attitude be towards them?

Take a minute to read back through 1 Corinthians 4:14–17. **¹What does Paul tell the Corinthians to do in verse 16? Why would Paul tell them to imitate him?**

Paul says to imitate him. It sounds like an arrogant statement. But Paul's getting at the same big idea we've been tackling so far in 1 Corinthians—choosing to risk our own interests and live the Spirit-led life.

Paul has already been living out the "foolish" life he's calling the Corinthians to imitate. He's given several examples throughout the first four chapters. In 1 Corinthians 4:8–13, he details how difficult it's been.

He's not saying, "Imitate me because I'm awesome." He's saying, "Follow my lead as I choose this crazy, upside-down life Jesus called us to." He desperately wants the Corinthians to give up their selfish act and embrace everything he's taught them about Jesus.

So here's what we can take away from Paul's words: We should learn from other Christians. We don't have to live exactly like they do. But we can apply the principles we learn from them to our lives. We do need to be careful to choose the right people—those who are actually choosing to live selflessly.

Who are some of the influential Christians in your life? What have they done to show you how to put other people before yourself?

We also need the right attitude. Other Christians aren't God. They aren't the ones causing us to grow. And they aren't to be used as weapons against other Christians.

Pick one of the people you listed in the previous question and take a few minutes to evaluate your attitude towards him or her. Have you idolized that person? If he or she were to leave your life today, how would it affect you?

As we imitate other Christians who are obedient to Jesus, the hope is that we'd also become role models for fellow believers. **As we close today, take some time to think about your life. Would you say you live in a way that's worth imitating? What if the people in your life—your friends, coworkers, or kids—acted just like you? Would they be more like Jesus? Write out a prayer to God about your answer. Ask him to help you live a life worth imitating.**

Day Four

As we've talked about our culture and the culture of Corinth this week, we've hit some hard topics. Something sinister sits at the root of each worldly issue, and Paul addresses it directly in the final paragraph of chapter 4.

Take a look at 1 Corinthians 4:18. **What does Paul call some of the Christians in Corinth? Why have they earned that label?**

Paul calls the Corinthians arrogant. They're arrogant because they're acting like Paul won't be coming any time soon to straighten out the church. They've achieved a kind of social status by advocating for certain leaders and wielding their so-called wisdom like a weapon. It's gone to their heads.

Like so many of the problems in our own lives and the world itself, it all comes down to power. The Corinthians had tasted power through their favorite teacher. They felt the rush of using knowledge to speak over other people in their church.

But Paul sees their power for what it is because he knows it's not sourced in God. Read through verses 19 and 20. Paul says he'll come against whatever power the Corinthians think they have. And he knows they'll lose. Why? Because the kingdom of God is about a different kind of power. Compared to the scraps the Corinthians had scrounged up, God's power is like a tank next to a paper clip. The paper clip doesn't stand a chance.

If we take an honest look at ourselves, we'll see our own love of power. Celebrities have authority, so we flock to them. The more we consume, the more we feel like we have control over our lives. We voice our opinions about Sunday morning services to feel like we have a say.

We might not realize it, but we can be power hungry.

Jennie reminded us in her teaching that being a Christian means our loyalties have changed. We're no longer about bumping up our power—or even another person's power. God's power should be our sole concern.

His power created the world. His power defeated death. His power saved us.

It saved you.

Take several minutes to think about God's power. If you're artistic, try writing a poem or drawing a picture that reflects how powerful God is. Or journal about the ways you might be pursuing your own power—or the power the world offers you—instead of God's.

Day Five

We're at the end of the week and we've come to a transition in 1 Corinthians. Beginning in chapter 5, Paul shifts his argument to talk about more specific ways the Corinthians' selfishness has affected the church. So far we've seen how their selfishness impacted their approach to certain leaders.

Like we talked about in session one, this book is a letter. It was meant to be read in one sitting. So we're going to take today to go back through Paul's argument in the first four chapters. We're going to read this part of the letter like it was meant to be read— all together.

Before we get started, take a minute to write out a one-sentence prayer asking the Holy Spirit to speak to you through his Word.

Put away any distractions—your phone, tablet, or computer. Settle in and open up your Bible to 1 Corinthians 1 and read all the way to the end of chapter 4. Consider reading it out loud to yourself as it would have been read to the Corinthian church. **After going through all four chapters, what did the Holy Spirit say to you?**

We read the Bible to encounter God. And when we encounter God, we should walk away changed. **Spend a few minutes writing out one tangible way you could respond to what you've just read in 1 Corinthians. Maybe it's pausing to think about how you talk about leaders in your church. Or maybe it's sacrificing a few hours on a Saturday to visit a church member in the hospital. Or it could be journaling about the ways you could be making church about you.**

Whatever it is, talk to God about it. Pray for the strength to put 1 Corinthians 1–4 into action this week. Thank God for what he's been teaching you.

Root Out Sin

We've made it all the way to chapter 5 in 1 Corinthians, which means we're at the first major turning point in the letter. So far, we've seen how the Corinthians' selfishness and devotion to their culture has brought division in the church. They've prioritized comfort, power, and loyalty to certain leaders over caring for each other.

As we move into chapter 5, we'll see that the core issue among the Corinthian people is still the same. They're still self-centered. We'll find out how their selfishness infected the church in more than one area.

Paul tackles a specific problem within the church in this chapter—sexual sin. While we might be tempted to brush this chapter off as only applying to that ancient church, we'll see that it's more relevant to us than we might think.

Paul argues that Christians should take habitual sins seriously because not only are they toxic to us as individuals, they're also toxic to the church. That's what we'll unpack in this session.

Throughout this week, we want to make sure we walk away:

• Knowing what it means to take sexual sin seriously in the context of the church and in our own lives.

• Feeling remorse over the sexual sin we've allowed to infect our lives and the church.

• Resolved to identify and turn away from our sexual sin and allow other Christians to encourage us to do so.

As always, hold those goals in your mind as we go through this week's study.

★ QUESTIONS FOR SMALL GROUP DISCUSSION

These questions come from the free Facilitator's Guide for *The Book of 1 Corinthians* on RightNow Media's website. If you're leading a group, download the Facilitator's Guide to help lead discussion on Jennie's teaching and the passage from 1 Corinthians.

1   WHAT'S THE PROBLEM PAUL ADDRESSES IN THIS CHAPTER? WHAT'S PAUL'S SOLUTION TO THE PROBLEM?

2   WHAT'S YOUR REACTION TO PAUL'S SOLUTION? DO YOU THINK IT'S TOO HARSH, TOO MILD, OR SOMEWHERE IN BETWEEN?

3   WHY DO YOU THINK PAUL TOOK SEXUAL SIN SO SERIOUSLY? WHAT DOES IT SAY ABOUT THE CHURCH—AND JESUS—WHEN WE DON'T ADDRESS SEXUAL SIN?

4   HOW DO YOU FEEL ABOUT LETTING OTHER CHRISTIANS CONFRONT YOU ABOUT YOUR SIN? IF YOU'VE ALREADY ALLOWED OTHER CHRISTIANS TO POINT OUT YOUR SIN, HOW DID YOU RESPOND?

5   WHAT'S ONE WAY YOU COULD BE PROACTIVE ABOUT CONFRONTING THE SIN IN YOUR LIFE THIS WEEK?

"

We are built to need each other, to need accountability.

"

Day One

Jennie said it well: We live in a sexualized culture. So much so that the church has started to have the same attitude towards sex as those outside Christianity. We can look a lot like the world.

The same was true for the Corinthian church— but to a worse degree. Not only were they accepting sexual practices that were outside God's boundaries, but they were also praising a man for incest. They were tolerating a kind of relationship that even pagans rejected.

The church didn't just resemble the world. It was worse than it.

This week's study in 1 Corinthians 5 will ask us to confront the sin in us and in the church. We're not always used to tackling sin head-on in the way Paul describes in this chapter. But before we go any further, let's ask why. Why do we avoid confronting sin?

Maybe because it's unpopular in our society to tell someone that what they're doing is wrong. We're told to tolerate people and their choices. Confronting sin in another Christian is also risky. It could cost you a friendship. It could be painful. It could also mean giving other people permission to confront your own sin. And that's scary.

How do you feel about letting other Christians confront you about your sin? What are you risking? If you've already allowed other Christians to do that, how did you respond the first time?

It feels safer to let sin lurk in our lives and the lives of other Christians. That way, no one has to really know us and we don't look intolerant.

But as Jennie said, we can't afford to let sin roam free. We have to deal with it. Not just for the sake of the people outside of Christianity looking in, but also for the sake of each other. Living the backwards-to-the-world life Jesus invites us into means we're members of a new family. And we need to take care of each other.

The point of this week's study isn't to leave us wallowing in our sin. Whenever we confront sin in our lives, it should draw us closer to Jesus who died to free us from that very sin. **So, to finish off today, spend a few minutes praising Jesus for what he's done for you through his life, death, and resurrection. Listen to a worship song, journal a prayer, or simply spend a few minutes in silence with God.**

Day Two

Christians tend to run to two extremes when it comes to sin. We either lean too heavily towards grace and let sin slide or we're hyper vigilant about sin and almost lose grace entirely. Where's the balance?

Open up your Bible and read 1 Corinthians 5:1–8. We set up the situation yesterday: A church member was in a relationship with his stepmother—something even the pagans of Corinth thought offensive.

Paul leaves no room for questioning in this passage. What the man is doing is wrong. Very wrong. So wrong that Paul wants him out of the church. In verses 6–8, he alludes to an Old Testament tradition to show the Corinthians why it's so important to weed out the sin from the church.

Let's take a look at what Paul's referring to in verses 6–8. **Flip back to Exodus and read Exodus 12:1–20. While you're reading, jot down what the blood of the Passover lamb did for the Israelites and what the Israelites were supposed to do with leaven, or yeast.**

There are two big parallels to note from Exodus 12. The first is that Paul calls Jesus our Passover lamb. He's reminding us of what Jesus's death means for us. He freed us from death. He brought us into God's family. He paid the consequence for our sin. Paul wants the church to remember why we take sin seriously. It's because our God did, which led to Jesus's death and our salvation.

God's grace isn't a free ticket to do whatever we want in life. We remove the sin from our lives because of the grace we have through Jesus. He hated sin. We should too.

The second parallel from Exodus 12 is that God didn't tell the Israelites to throw leaven out of their houses just for fun. He had a purpose behind it: to prepare them to celebrate, remember, and enjoy the freedom he gave them from slavery in Egypt.

God doesn't ask us to remove sin from our lives without a reason.

Sometimes we focus so much on saying no to our sin that we forget what we're saying yes to when we turn away from sinful habits. Repenting of sin is more than turning your back on sin. It's also about what you turn toward—about what you get to experience because you've let go of sin.

So when it comes to finding a balance between being hyper-vigilant or too gracious about sin, we can start by remembering the grace God's already given us through Jesus. When we say no to sin, we're saying yes to grace. To love. To freedom. We experience true life when we put death behind us.

Imagine what a life completely free from sin would look like. How would your friendships change? Your self-talk? Your attitude at work? Take some time to reflect and journal about the life you say yes to when you reject sin.

Day Three

Yesterday we looked at two reactions we tend to have toward sin—letting it slide or focusing on it too much. Paul advocates for balance. As those who have received God's grace, we need to take sin seriously.

Read 1 Corinthians 5:9–13. **According to Paul, whom should Christians avoid? How does that sit with you?**

Paul doesn't beat around the bush. He says the church should not associate with sexually immoral people who claim to be Christians. In verse 11, he broadens the command to include many more types of Christians.

So, does that mean we can't hang out with anyone? We all have some sort of sin we're dealing with, right?

Paul isn't saying we should avoid all people with sin in their life. For one, he goes out of his way to say he's not talking about non-Christians. We should hang around people who don't know Jesus. That's often how people become Christians.

But he's also not saying shun someone who slips up once or who actively seeks help with a sin problem. We all mess up. It's part of being human. The beauty of being a member of the family of God comes when we help each other turn away from sin and toward God.

But part of membership in God's family is that we, together, live like Jesus. That means we don't tolerate persistent, unrepentant, habitual sin. People who actively rebel against God will damage the church.

It's as if you are holding hands in a line of ten people and one person tries to pull the group in a different direction—the line could eventually split apart or change its course.

That's why Paul wants the Corinthians to be proactive about this man's unrepentant sin. It's for the sake of the entire group of Christians and it's for the benefit of the man—a wakeup call could bring him around.

It's all a part of the backwards-to-the-world life Paul's been talking about in 1 Corinthians. As Jennie said in the video, the church should be different. If we hold each other to Jesus's standard, we stand out.

So how are you doing with all of this? Does Paul's aggressiveness toward sin bother you? Or is it more normal to you? **Close your time today in prayer. Express what you're feeling to God. Ask him questions. And then take five minutes to listen to him**.

Day Four

We've been looking at why Paul takes sin so seriously in this chapter of 1 Corinthians. It can cause serious damage in the church. Paul wants sin cleaned out. This chapter rubs against everything we see as normal and right in our culture. It's not politically correct to tell someone they're sinning, let alone kick them out for doing something wrong. And, as Christians, we often look to the several Bible passages that tell us not to judge each other.

So, which is it? Do we judge or not?

Open up your Bible and read 1 Corinthians 5:12–13. Paul's words at the end of this chapter can be confusing. He tells the Corinthians to judge each other on their sin. But Paul said the Corinthians weren't supposed to judge at the beginning of chapter 4. So when is it okay to judge?

Peek at the Greek

The Greek word for "judge," *krinō*, carries legal undertones, much like our word does in English. It means to determine if something is right or wrong or if a person is guilty or not guilty. One way to think about the word *krinō* is as arriving at a verdict. We sometimes read the word "judge" and think about being critical of someone or condemning them, whether through our thoughts or words. But Paul's simply talking about figuring out what is right or wrong by God's standards. In this case, the church should consider if the man in question is acting in accordance with God's law or not.

When Paul tells the Corinthians not to judge in chapter 4, he's saying they shouldn't try to determine the validity of his apostolic ministry because God's the one to do that. He's not talking about judging sin. In chapter 5, Paul's saying the church should be aware of and proactive against habitual sin in its members.

As members of God's family, we have to take care of each other. That means we do everything we can to make sure the whole family stays healthy. Kicking someone out of the church can seem harsh to us. But it's the one of the ways the church can stay healthy. And it's often the only way someone can realize the consequence for their sin and turn back to God.

You might recall Jesus's words about judging others—Jennie even mentioned them in her teaching. He says to make sure you deal with your own problems before pointing them out in other people. His words apply here. We shouldn't go around condemning other Christians for their sin when we have unrepentant sin in our own lives. Calling out sin should always begin in us.

That doesn't mean we're the first ones to call out other people's sin. Rather, we open ourselves up to the judgment of others. We live transparently. We create so much stress for ourselves by trying to hide our sin. But if we're open about our struggles, we can live free—free from the burden of hiding it and free from the guilt and shame of it.

Imagine what your life could be like if you were completely transparent about your sin. Sure, it'd be scary at first. But you'd never have to worry about being caught. You'd never be caught off guard if someone called you out on your sin. You'd be free.

Take a moment to reflect on this question: **What's keeping you from living that way now?**

Day Five

We've come to the end of a difficult chapter. Paul doesn't mess around when it comes to sin. He takes it seriously and we should too. We finished yesterday reflecting on the ways we could be misjudging the other Christians around us.

Today, we're taking a hard look in the mirror. Like we talked about yesterday, calling out the sins in other people begins in us. So we're going to invite the Holy Spirit to do some work.

Find some time today to be alone, without distractions. It could be five minutes. It could be an hour. Turn off your phone. Put your computer out of sight. And be silent.

¹Start off by thanking God for what he's done for you through Jesus. Think about Jesus's gruesome death and miraculous resurrection. Thank God for ending the war against death.

★ ACROCORINTH

Also known simply as the acropolis of Corinth, this area housed a temple to the goddess Aphrodite. Her role in Greek mythology as the goddess of love and sex is importance for understanding the context of Corinth, one known for its sexual immorality and prostitution.

Then ask the Spirit to show you the sin that's crept into your life. As he shows you, confess it to God. Pray for tangible ways to turn away from that sin. If there's something habitual—like what Paul talks about in this chapter—ask God to direct you toward help.

Close by asking God for strength to choose an others-centered life despite the risk. Tell him any fears you have about confronting the sin in your life and in the lives of others. Pray that he would guide you in being both gracious and truthful.

After the Spirit shows you some of the sin in your life, you might feel overwhelmed. You might want to give up. You might think you'll never change. If that's you, grab a Christian friend and tell them what God just revealed to you. Confess your sin. Pray together.

We were never meant to do this Christian life alone. We need each other. Together, we walk hand-in-hand toward Jesus.

Set Aside Selfishness

Last week we examined what it looks like to deal with sin in this others-centered life we've been exploring in 1 Corinthians. Paul advocates for taking sin seriously—for uprooting it in the church and in us. We must be proactive about anything that poisons the church to keep it healthy.

Chapter 5 asked us to get rid of things we know to be wrong and shouldn't be doing—things that even those outside Christianity think are wrong. As we move into chapter 6 this week, Paul will challenge us to give up things the world deems okay, such as getting justice through a lawsuit or going outside of marriage for sex.

Jesus modeled a life for us that always set selfishness aside for the sake of others. He asks us to imitate that life. Being like Jesus doesn't mean just saying no to the things everyone already thinks are wrong. It also involves saying no to what everyone outside of Christianity may think is okay but actually violates God, hurts other Christians, and destroys us.

That's the big idea we'll explore in this session, and by studying that idea we want to:

• Know that the others-centered life means we set aside selfishness for the sake of others and ourselves.

• Feel compelled to choose selflessness like Jesus did when it comes to sexual desires and lawsuits.

• Risk getting hurt by other Christians and risk unfulfilled sexual desire.

A life that follows Jesus is risky because it's so different from the world. But being like Jesus is also what sets us apart. It's what makes us like a city lit-up at night.

These questions come from the free Facilitator's Guide for *The Book of 1 Corinthians* on RightNow Media's website. If you're leading a group, download the Facilitator's Guide to help lead discussion on Jennie's teaching and the passage from 1 Corinthians.

1   WHAT'S PAUL SAYING ABOUT LAWSUITS AND SEXUAL DESIRES IN THIS CHAPTER?

2   WHAT THOUGHTS AND ATTITUDES WOULD YOU HAVE TO DEAL WITH IN YOURSELF IF A CHRISTIAN WRONGED YOU? WHAT DO YOU THINK YOU'D DO IN THAT SITUATION?

3   WHAT DIFFERENCE DOES IT MAKE IN THE WAY YOU THINK ABOUT YOURSELF AND OTHERS TO KNOW THAT YOUR BODY ISN'T YOUR OWN—IT'S CHRIST'S?

4   WHEN HAVE YOU HAD TO PUT YOUR DESIRES ASIDE FOR THE SAKE OF ANOTHER PERSON? HOW DID YOU FEEL IN THE MOMENT? WHAT DID YOU LEARN?

5   WHAT'S ONE TANGIBLE WAY YOU COULD CHOOSE TO BE SELFLESS THIS WEEK TOWARD ONE PERSON IN YOUR LIFE?

"

We've been bought with a price. We belong to Christ.

"

Day One

Last week's study had us looking at sin practices that even repulsed the Corinthians outside of the church. This week is a little different. We're going to look at two things both the secular Corinthians and the Christians did—taking people to court and more "acceptable" sexual immorality.

Grab your Bible. Open up to 1 Corinthians 6 and read the whole chapter. [1]**As you read, look out for three things and write them down: What Jesus has done for us in the past, the present consequences for our actions, and finally what God will do in the future.**

Jennie hit on past, present, and future reasons why we should reject actions and attitudes the world thinks are okay.

We should first reject the world's ways because of what Jesus did for us through his life, death, and resurrection. Verse 11 reminds us of all we received because of Jesus. He blots out the permanent stains of sin. He sets us apart as members of his family. And he removes the guilty verdict that hangs over our heads.

What Jesus has done for us should radically change us today. But that's not the only reason for living differently from the world as we know it. Jennie talked about the consequences we face when we compromise and act like everyone else. We cause division. We hurt other people. We personally suffer.

Jennie also reminded us of the future hope we have through Jesus. Paul hints at it in verses 2 and 14—when Jesus returns, God will raise us from the dead and we will rule in the new earth. Jesus will return and hit the refresh button on creation. The earth will be brand new and we will reign with Jesus.

There are so many good reasons for us to decide to live in a way that's different from the rest of the world. The question is whether or not those reasons are enough for you.

Thinking through the past, present, and future reasons Jenny mentioned, which is most compelling to you as a reason to risk living other-centered? Spend some time journaling about how that reason equips you to handle the world's view on sex and lawsuits. What does it look like to combat the world's ideology with a Christ-centered hope?

Following Jesus involves a great exchange: your life for his. He asks us to give up everything. But in return, he gives us everything.

Is that enough for you?

1

2

★ CONSIDER THIS

Before we dive into today's study, it's important to note what this passage is *not* saying. It's not advocating for settling all legal matters only within the church. Paul tells the church on several occasions to submit to the Roman law and to allow Christians to experience the full consequence of that law—he even did so himself. That means if there is ever any illegal activity within the church such as domestic violence, rape, or abuse, the church should always go to the authorities. Paul urges the church to act in a way that's against the cultural norm. Bringing sin to light under the authority of the law is one of the most counter-cultural things the church can do.

Day Two

Have you ever felt embarrassed by someone? Maybe your kid threw a fit in the grocery story the other day. Or maybe your friend said something offensive at a dinner party without knowing it. We've all felt the shrink-into-your-seat feeling when someone does something that disrupts the norm.

That feeling only scratches the surface of what Paul's expressing in the first part of chapter 6. Look back at verses 1–8. Paul is furious with the way the Christians in Corinth are acting. Instead of settling their personal matters within the church, they're dragging other Christians through legal battles that were often corrupt. In other words, they're being completely selfish.

The big issue Paul's dealing with pops up in verse 6. He's concerned about how the Corinthians are acting in front of people who don't believe in Jesus. Outsiders look at the church and see people arguing, sleeping with whomever they choose, and taking each other to court.

That doesn't reflect well on Jesus.

How the church appears to the outside world matters. The way we treat each other shows others who Jesus is. When we fight each other, demand money from each other, or sue each other, it tells outsiders that being part of the family isn't different than staying out of it.

Today we face the same tension the Corinthians faced. In a culture that's more and more polarizing, especially in the United States, Christians can either throw punches like the rest of the world or choose to hang up the boxing gloves and leave the ring. [1]**What are some sources of division you've encountered in your church?**

[2]If you have social media, take five minutes today to scroll through your personal profiles and feeds. What do you see? What kind of comments do you leave? Are you causing dissonance? Or are you promoting peace between other Christians?

Internal disputes can be settled within the church. But it has to begin with us. We can treat each other well in public, whether that be online or in person. We have to be the first ones to put aside selfishness and risk getting hurt by selfish people in the process.

Take a few minutes to reflect on the conversations you have with other Christians, particularly in your local church. [3]What could you do this week to promote unity through the way you talk to and about the other members of your church?

Does the way you treat other Christians in public reflect Jesus? Or the world?

1

2

3

Day Three

We left yesterday with the conclusion that treating other Christians poorly sends a bad message to the world about who Jesus is and what it means to be part of his family. But what are we supposed to do if another Christian cheats us? In 1 Corinthians 6:7, Paul has an answer: It's better for us to be wronged and cheated than to wrong and cheat others.

Wait. Is Paul saying we should allow other Christians to walk all over us? Not necessarily. The relational and financial wisdom we find in the book of Proverbs and elsewhere in Scripture warns against acting foolishly. Paul's getting at living the backwards life we've been talking about in this study.

The life Jesus invites us to live is risky. We've been saying that all throughout this book. It's risky because it's different from the world, yes. But it goes much deeper than that. It's risky because it asks us to put our own safety, security, and comfort on the line. It asks us to be open to being hurt by other believers.

When we put other people first, they will let us down. It happened for Jesus. It will happen for us if it hasn't already.

The big question is why. Why risk it all for people who might hurt us?

It all comes back to Jesus. Read 1 Corinthians 6:7–11. Paul reminds the Corinthians of who they used to be before Jesus. They were sexually immoral, idolaters, thieves, slanderers, and swindlers. Paul's saying that behavior has no room in the kingdom of God. When the Corinthians revert back to those actions, they're acting as if Jesus hadn't done anything.

Paul circles back in verse 11 to point out that, through Jesus, the stains from their past and the separation from God are gone. We have gained so much and verse 11 only scratches the surface. We often jump to the benefits we receive through Jesus and forget how he achieved those things for us.

Take five minutes to skim through Mark 14—a passage that falls right before Jesus goes to the cross. Think about Jesus's life and death. He lived a difficult life. The religious elite mocked and threatened him. His disciples abandoned him when he needed them the most. The Romans abused and killed him. But Jesus let it happen. He let people hurt him.

Why? Because of us. He was more concerned about saving us than keeping himself safe.

Paul asks Christians to take a risk—to put other people first, even if it costs us. We don't take the risk alone. We mimic the footsteps of Jesus who went before us.

Day Four

Yesterday had us considering what it could look like to risk getting hurt for the sake of other people. Without Jesus, few people would really think about putting their safety and security on the line for other people. And we're not done yet.

In the rest of chapter 6, Paul tackles another thing people rarely deny themselves—sex.

We've already covered how promiscuous the Corinthian culture was. People flocked to temple prostitutes, men had multiple wives, and the general population erred on the side of pleasure.

The world today isn't much different from the Corinthians. Sexual pleasure still rules the day. It pops up in our ads, TV shows, books, movies, and conversations. Porn, sex abuse, and affairs don't startle us anymore. They're just part of everyday life. It's tragic, but true.

Read 1 Corinthians 6:12–20. Paul's words in this passage are harsh and grotesque because the Corinthians' actions are harsh and grotesque. Sexual immorality has no place among God's people. Jesus paid everything for us. Our lives—and our bodies—are now his. Turning to sexual sin is like smacking Jesus in the face.

So, Paul says to flee.

12 "All things are lawful for me," but not all things are helpful. "All things are lawful for me," but I will not be dominated by anything. 13 "Food is meant for the stomach and the stomach for food"—and God will destroy both one and the other. The body is not meant for sexual immorality, but for the Lord, and the Lord for the body. 14 And God raised the Lord and will also raise us up by his power. 15 Do you not know that your bodies are members of Christ? Shall I then take the members of Christ and make them members of a prostitute? Never! 16 Or do you not know that he who is joined to a prostitute becomes one body with her? For, as it is written, "The two will become one flesh." 17 But he who is joined to the Lord becomes one spirit with him. 18 Flee from sexual immorality. Every other sin a person commits is outside the body, but the sexually immoral person sins against his own body. 19 Or do you not know that your body is a temple of the Holy Spirit within you, whom you have from God? You are not your own, 20 for you were bought with a price. So glorify God in your body.

1 CORINTHIANS 6:12–20

He even goes as far to say that when we engage in any type of sexual immorality, we bring Christ with us. He uses the example of uniting Jesus with a prostitute to shock the Corinthians. **What's your reaction to Paul's example? In your own words, what's Paul saying about the Corinthians' actions through this choice of illustration?**

The Corinthians' actions defile Jesus. The church. Themselves.

Our culture argues for pleasure, acceptance, and romantic love wherever it can be found. As Jesus's people, though, we keep sex within the good bounds God has set for it—marriage. It's not easy and people outside the church think we're crazy.

We have to take sexual sin seriously. We cannot let it seep into our lives. If we allow it in, it only brings destruction.

Spend the next few minutes journaling through the following questions.

Where do you see sexual temptation at play in your life? When is it the most tempting? What tempts you the most?

What could it look like for you to flee sexual immorality? What kinds of steps could you take to weed out any sexual sin in your life?

Remember the big idea Paul's advocating for in 1 Corinthians—Christians need each other. If you're struggling with an habitual sexual sin, get help. Tell a trusted Christian friend. Find support through your church. The Christian life is risky, but it's not a solo journey.

1

2

3

Day Five

We've come to the end of another difficult passage in 1 Corinthians. So, for this final day, we're going to take a step back. Chapter 6 demands a lot from us. It asks us to act in a way that contradicts everything the world stands for.

That's what it means to be a Christian. It requires us to make tough decisions—decisions that look foolish to the world. It looks like not cheating other people out of money. It's deciding against having an affair. It means getting help with our porn addiction.

It's one thing to talk about what Paul's asking us to do in this passage. It's another thing entirely to actually do it.

So as this week closes, we're going to try to put Paul's words into action. To do it, we're going to use one of the spiritual disciplines, which is just a fancy phrase for practices that help us grow closer to God. The one we'll be using is called fasting.

Fasting is a way of denying ourselves something we normally enjoy—such as food, TV, or social media—for a short period of time. Jennie mentioned fasting in her teaching. She said it should be a joyful choice we make. It's only for a little bit of time, but it's a way we can refocus our priorities.

If we're honest, fasting is one more thing that looks crazy to the world. No one willingly chooses to give up something they see as essential to living. But we're going to give it a try as a way of living out the risky, backwards-to-the-world life.

Pick one thing to give up. Maybe it's the internet or desserts or a few meals. Try avoiding that thing or habit for one whole day. Whenever you feel the urge to eat a piece of cake or scroll through Facebook, pray instead. Ask God to give you the strength to say no. Tell him what you're feeling. Thank him for three things he's given you. Use your hunger pains to help reorient your mind toward God.

Then come back to this page and write about your experience. What did giving up your one thing feel like? What was difficult for you? What did you learn?

Keep Station

Reading 1 Corinthians feels like watching Paul take the Corinthians on a walk through their problems and we're just along for the ride. It's similar to taking a guided tour through an art museum. The guide plants you in front of painting after painting, pointing out different things you might not have noticed on your own.

So far, Paul's discussed several areas where the Corinthians were messing up—leadership, sexuality, and lawsuits. Though Paul's talking about ancient problems in an ancient church, their issues are similar—if not the same—to the ones we experience today.

The same goes for this week's chapter. Paul will ask us to reassess how we approach our romantic relationships—whether we're single, married, widowed, divorced, or engaged. The bottom line is that romance and relationships were never meant to satisfy us. We have much, much more to live for. We can be faithful to God where he's placed us while also being hopeful for the future. And that's what we'll be talking about in this week's trek through 1 Corinthians 7.

No matter your relationship status, this session is for you. Through studying 1 Corinthians 7, we want to:

- Know what it means to be selfless in the context of our romantic relationships.

- Feel excited about God's purpose for relationships and the future hope we have in Jesus's return.

- Look for ways to put other people first, regardless of our relationship status.

With those goals in mind, let's dive into chapter 7.

WATCH SESSION 6
THE BOOK OF 1 CORINTHIANS
WITH JENNIE ALLEN

★ QUESTIONS FOR SMALL GROUP DISCUSSION

These questions come from the free Facilitator's Guide for *The Book of 1 Corinthians* on RightNow Media's website. If you're leading a group, download the Facilitator's Guide to help lead discussion on Jennie's teaching and the passage from 1 Corinthians.

1   WHAT LIFE STAGE ARE YOU IN RIGHT NOW? WHAT'S BEST ABOUT IT? WHAT ARE SOME DIFFICULTIES?

2   WHAT'S PAUL'S MAIN MESSAGE ABOUT OUR VARIOUS LIFE STAGES? AFTER JENNIE'S TEACHING AND READING 1 CORINTHIANS 7, WHAT DO YOU THINK IT MEANS TO "KEEP STATION"?

3   WHAT DOES CONTENTMENT LOOK LIKE FOR YOU? WHAT HELPS YOU FIND THAT CONTENTMENT EVEN IN DIFFICULT SITUATIONS?

4   THINK ABOUT THE WAY YOU TREAT THE SIGNIFICANT PEOPLE IN YOUR LIFE. WHAT DO YOU THINK YOUR ACTIONS TOWARDS THEM SAY TO OTHER PEOPLE ABOUT YOUR FAITH?

5   WHAT'S ONE THING YOU COULD DO TO SELFLESSLY SERVE A SIGNIFICANT PERSON IN YOUR LIFE THIS WEEK?

"

Wherever God has placed you, be all there.

"

Day One

We grow up always looking for what's next. It starts in grade school. We long for next year's teacher or a locker or graduation. Then we look forward to getting a degree, finding a spouse, or having kids. It's easy to be dissatisfied with where we are right now.

Chapter 7 is about marriage, singleness, and everything in between. Paul wants the Corinthians to apply the selfless Christian life to their relationships. He tackles the desire we all have to obsess over what's coming instead of what's in front of us.

[1] **So before we dive into this chapter, take few minutes to reflect on your current life stage, specifically when it comes to romantic relationships. Are you single? Married? Divorced? Widowed? Would you say you're happy with your relationship status? What's most difficult about where you are right now? The most exciting?**

Space to write on the next page... **135**

With your answer in mind, grab your Bible and read all of 1 Corinthians 7. **While you're reading, jot down any observations you make about your current life stage. Write down any questions you might have about those verses.**

Jennie hit on our big idea for this session in the video: Keep your station. In other words, live faithfully in the life stage God's placed you in. That's what we're going to unpack in the next four days— what it means to be present and others-focused wherever God's placed us.

There's a lot to cover in these forty verses. No matter if you're married or single, there's something for you in this chapter. If your questions don't get answered through this week's study, talk with a trusted Christian friend or pastor.

1

2

Day Two

We talk a lot about personal rights in today's world—especially in the United States. Culture says we're owed sexual fulfillment. We're entitled to romance.

But what God says about sex and relationships is entirely different. If we follow Paul's logic from the rest of 1 Corinthians, relationships—as with everything else in the Christian life—should be entirely others-centered. Relationships aren't about us.

That's a completely different message from what we hear. Romance is supposed to make us happy. It's supposed to leave us sexually satisfied. It's supposed to make us feel secure.

Except, Paul says it's not. Because relationships aren't about you.

Read back through what Paul writes in 1 Corinthians 7:1–9. His words would have shocked the Corinthians who lived in a culture where marriage was primarily about legal standing and sexual fulfillment for men. Women didn't matter. They got married to avoid poverty, to please their fathers, or to keep from public shame.

Paul steps in and flips the cultural idea of marriage on its head. In just a few verses, Paul shatters the conventional view of marriage the Corinthians had—and the one we might have ourselves. He says marriage should serve the other person.

That's a good message for married and single people alike. If you have a spouse, he or she is not built to satisfy you. They can't. Our goal in marriage shouldn't be to live happily ever after. It should be to care for, listen to, and meet the needs of your spouse. Of course the hope is that you and your spouse would serve each other and both of you would have your needs met. But it's not guaranteed. And it's not something you're owed. Marriage is a risk.

And, if you aren't married, hold on to this truth: Marriage is not the end game. It will not fulfill you. It can't. Your life isn't about your pleasure or joy or relationship status. It's about God. It's about his people.

We're back to talking about the risky, others-centered life again. It's terrifying to focus only on your spouse in marriage. What if your needs don't get met? It's also scary to let go of a romanticized view of marriage. What if daydreams are the closest you'll ever get to saying "I do"?

How does Paul's concept of marriage and singleness sit with you? Spend the next five minutes in prayer. Talk to God about the worries you have about being married or single. Ask him all your questions. And then listen to his voice.

1

★ CONSIDER THIS

You might notice that we haven't talked about divorce extensively in this study. That's on purpose. Like Jennie said in the video, it's best discussed in the context of your local church. If you have questions, talk with the leaders of your church about how they handle this passage.

Day Three

There's an idea among Christians that says you're only a really good Christian if you do certain things for God—like be a missionary in an impoverished country or sell your suburban house to live in the inner city. While living radically for Jesus can be a good, God-ordained thing for some people, making it a universal mandate can also create unnecessary pressure and lead us away from actual obedience.

There's a huge difference between doing something because God led you to do it and doing something because you felt like you had to. That's what Paul's getting at in the verses we'll study today.

Go back through 1 Corinthians 7:10–24. The people in the church thought they could do whatever they wanted—leave their marriages, force people to get circumcised, or willingly become a slave to pay off debts. **[1]What do you think motivated the Corinthians to make these decisions? How could selfishness be involved?**

Instead of being selfish, Paul challenged the Corinthians to remain where they were. It's a thought that completely goes against the Christian norm even today. Instead of telling people to chase their passions, leap into vocational ministry, or move across the Mediterranean to a new city, Paul says, "Stay where you are."

If you're in a marriage with an unbeliever, stay. If you're in a job that's hard right now, stay. If you're in a family full of tension, stay.

That's not to say that there aren't healthy reasons to leave a job or marriage or city. There are. But Paul wants us to default to steady, enduring faithfulness. It should be our first response.

Staying isn't sexy. It's hard. The issues Paul talks about in this passage are rough. He's not painting the Christian life as easy. It's still risky. It could still hurt. Being a Christian is much less about big adventures than it is about everyday obedience. Jesus asks us to obey him where he's placed us— whether it's as a parent of four, a grocery story clerk, or a pastor of a small church. One life situation isn't better or worse than the other. Obedience is what matters.

[2] **Think about your job, relationships, church. Pick the one that you're most uncomfortable "staying" in. What would it look like for you to dig in your heels and persist in that area of your life?**

Talk to God about your answer. If you're wrestling with the idea of staying— especially in a less-than-ideal situation—tell him. Pray for the strength to obey, even when it's hard.

What Jennie said in the video about abuse applies to this passage. Paul is not telling wives and husbands to stay in a marriage that brings physical or emotional harm to them or anyone else. If you are in an abusive relationship, get help. Contact the police. If you're in the United States, call the Domestic Abuse Hotline at 1-800-799-7233.

1

2

Day Four

So far this week, we've been talking about staying where God has placed us—whether that's as a spouse or a single person. Our romantic relationships and our life stage aren't about us, but we often think they are.

But today we hit a passage near the end of the chapter that seems to contradict everything we've looked at so far. Read 1 Corinthians 7:29–31.

On the surface, it seems like Paul is saying the present world is passing away, which means we should live as if we aren't in our current life stage. But we have to take this passage in context with the rest of the chapter. Re-read verses 25–28.

Paul is talking directly to people who are unmarried and who haven't been married before. He goes out of his way to make it clear that what he's saying isn't a command. It's just his pastoral advice. He's telling single adults that their time might be better spent if they stay unmarried.

So when we get to verse 29, Paul's still addressing the never-married crowd. He reminds them that this life is short. We should spend our time wisely. In Paul's eyes, the wisest way forward for a single person is to continue to be single and to commit every day to God without being bogged down with the worries of the world.

Paul's adding to what he's already been saying about relationships. They aren't about us and we should live well in the relationships God has placed us in. But that's not the end of the story.

Our days on earth are numbered. But Jesus will return one day, raise us to life, and usher us into eternity. We live today in light of that hope. Paul wants the Corinthians to know why we stay in marriages with unbelievers or remain celibate as single adults. It's because there's a future on the horizon for us in Jesus. The present world won't last. We're living for one that will.

[1] **Close your eyes for a few minutes. Picture one of the most beautiful places you've ever seen. Now try to make the image in your mind even more stunning—add flowers, make the sun shine brighter, scent the air with pine trees. Sit in that image for a while. Write it down.**

In the closing pages of the Bible, John describes eternity as a new heaven and a new earth. We aren't waiting for some pew-bound, never-ending worship service. Newness is coming. What you just pictured in your mind is closer to what eternity will look like than white robes and harps. That's the image Paul wanted the Corinthians to look forward to. We live faithfully today while also holding tightly to the hope that is to come.

1

Day Five

As we wrap up our study of chapter 7, let's remind ourselves of what Paul is not saying. He's not saying it's bad to be married or even to get married. He's also not saying all Christians should stay or become single. He's simply pointing out what it means to be faithfully obedient in specific life stages.

It's easy to idolize another life stage. We can make romantic relationships a kind of god. We can make singleness god. As we've discussed through this week's study, the goal of every Christian should be to live well—to obey—wherever God has placed us. That means choosing celibacy if we're single. It means caring for our spouse if we're married. It means longing for eternity instead of obsessing over a different relationship status.

To finish off this week, we're going to spend some time talking to God. [1]**Start off with some honest talk about the life stage you're in right now. Are you happy with it? Are you frustrated with God? What would you prefer instead?**

[2]**Then tell him what you expect from relationships—whether it's security, comfort, or companionship. Ask God to show you if you're being selfish with your relationships. Confess anything he brings up.**

[3]**End your time in prayer by asking God to show you one way you can live out this passage in your life this week. Write down that one thing. Come back to this page in a few days and write about how trying it out went.**

1

2

3

Turn From Pride

We're at the halfway point in 1 Corinthians. Since the beginning of this study, we've walked through Paul's frustrations with the Corinthians' actions. In chapter 5 we talked about sin practices that even non-Christians deplore. In chapters 6 and 7, Paul spoke about actions the world accepts but Christians should not pursue. Now as we dive into chapter 8, Paul will hit on some of the gray areas of Christianity—the practices some Christians approve of and others don't.

We're also going to encounter an overarching argument both in this session and the next. Paul's going to unpack the issue of sacrificing meat to idols—a custom that couldn't be more different from what we experience today. While the cultural divide might seem too wide to bridge, we'll find in this session and the session that follows that the principles from this passage still apply to us today.

We'll hit on the main idea of spiritual maturity and how it should affect us as Christians. If we're going to live a selfless life, then the longer we follow Jesus the more humble and self-sacrificing we should become. Being grown up, knowledgeable, or experienced in the Christian life shouldn't puff up our pride—it should make us more like Jesus.

Through this session, we want to:

- Recognize the areas of pride in our own lives, particularly when it comes to other Christians.

- Feel humility in light of our areas of weakness.

- Reject certain practices that could cause other Christians to sin.

These questions come from the free Facilitator's Guide for *The Book of 1 Corinthians* on RightNow Media's website. If you're leading a group, download the Facilitator's Guide to help lead discussion on Jennie's teaching and the passage from 1 Corinthians.

1   WHAT RESONATED WITH YOU FROM JENNIE'S ILLUSTRATION ABOUT HER SONS? WHEN HAVE YOU FELT LIKE THE OLDER SON? THE YOUNGER?

2   WHAT MAKES THE CORINTHIANS' ACTIONS IN THIS CHAPTER PRIDEFUL? WHERE DO YOU SEE A PRIDEFUL ATTITUDE IN YOUR LIFE?

3   WHAT ARE SOME GRAY AREAS WHERE YOU MIGHT HAVE TO "PLAY AT THE LEVEL" OF OTHER CHRISTIANS?

4   HOW WOULD YOU FEEL IF SOMEONE SET ASIDE ONE OF THEIR RIGHTS FOR YOUR BENEFIT? WHAT KIND OF A DIFFERENCE WOULD IT MAKE IN YOUR RELATIONSHIP WITH THAT PERSON?

5   WHAT COULD IT LOOK LIKE FOR YOU TO CHOOSE HUMILITY THIS WEEK? COULD YOU SET ASIDE A RIGHT? MEET ANOTHER CHRISTIAN'S NEEDS? CONFESS SIN?

"

We're loved and known by God. That should humble us.

"

★ ANCIENT CORINTH (NEAR BEMA SEAT)

A "bema" was an elevated platform where officials would carry out judicial decisions among the legal center of a city. The bema of Corinth is likely where Paul was brought before Gallio in Acts 18:12–17.

Day One

As we grow up, we must answer this question: Will we use our experience, knowledge, and expertise as an adult to help others or ourselves?

Jennie used the example of her two sons to show that, as we mature, it doesn't necessarily give us free reign to wield our power or strength or understanding over those who aren't as far along as we are. Growing up should mean we give up certain things for the sake of others.

[1] **What resonated with you from Jennie's illustration about her sons? When have you felt like the older son? The younger?**

As Christians, we encounter the same question—will we use our spiritual maturity for others or for ourselves?

If we choose to live for ourselves, the inevitable result is pride. We begin to think our knowledge of God or our way of living the Christian life is better—or even the best. That's what the Corinthians had fallen into. We've seen it all throughout the book. Their pride comes to the surface in a whole new way in the chapter we'll be studying this week. Their actions are now leading other people to sin. It's a big deal.

But there is another way. It's what we've been talking about through this entire study. We can use any wisdom or growth in our Christian lives to help other Christians. We can take the self-sacrificing route of humility—the road Jesus trekked.

That's what we'll dig into this week—the choice we have between pride and humility and how our choice affects other Christians.

[2] **Close your time today by wrestling with this question: Where does pride pop up in your life? Take a virtual journey through a typical day in your life and ask God to show you where pride takes center stage. Ask him to soften your heart to what he has to teach you through this week's study.**

Day Two

This week's passage will draw us into the culture of Corinth yet again. So, before we jump into the text, let's get a little background.

As we've said before, Corinth had temples for many gods, and one of the common practices of the day was offering sacrifices to those gods. They often offered up meat from various animals.

The priests in these temples were allowed to eat the sacrificed meat for their daily meals. With thousands of people bringing in food on a daily basis, however, there was always plenty leftover. The wealthier people who sacrificed the meat could reclaim it and serve it to their friends and family. Some meat was also sold in the market.

The Corinthians evidently had an ongoing debate about whether or not it was okay to eat the meat that had been sacrificed to false gods. Some felt fine about enjoying the food with friends and family, seeing it as Christ-given freedom. Others saw it as participating in the idolatrous worship of other gods.

That's what Paul's addressing in 1 Corinthians 8. Open up your Bible and read the entire chapter with this information in mind.

Summarize the problem Paul identifies in your own words. What's going on? Who's in the wrong?

While it might feel like this chapter has nothing to do with us today, Paul's pointing out a heart issue that still applies to us. The Corinthians were prideful. The ones who thought it was okay to eat the meat didn't see the harm their actions were causing. And those who condemned eating the sacrificed meat judged those who did.

As we introduced yesterday, people on both sides of the issue were prideful. Neither group was living in the others-centered way Paul's been advocating throughout his letter.

Today, we can also get wrapped up in pride, especially when it comes to how to live the Christian life. We can hold on to certain dos and don'ts—such as drinking alcohol, watching certain TV shows and movies, wearing certain clothing, spending our money in a specific way, or adhering to a certain political party. When we refuse to let go of certain non-gospel issues, it can tear a rift between us and other Christians.

Go back through 1 Corinthians 8. This time, look for the hints of pride in the Corinthians' actions and words—especially toward each other. Write down what you observe. Then spend a few minutes in prayer to ask God where pride could be showing up in your life.

We'll dig into the issue of pride this week. Pray God would open your eyes to the areas of pride in your life.

1

2

Day Three

It's a great feeling when we know something someone else doesn't. Whether it's the best route to a burger joint, the proper way to change a tire, or the name of the president of Turkey, pride bubbles up in us when our knowledge surpasses everyone else's.

The same pride can show up in us as Christians—it certainly had for the Corinthians. Flip to 1 Corinthians 8 and read verses 1 to 6. [1]**What "knowledge" had the Corinthians learned? What effect did it have on them?**

Many of the Corinthians knew that idols weren't real. There's only one God. All other gods are false. But that knowledge had puffed up their pride. We'll talk about the external consequences for their pride tomorrow. Today we'll focus in the internal destruction pride can have on us.

Now concerning food offered to idols: we know that "all of us possess knowledge." This "knowledge" puffs up, but love builds up. ² If anyone imagines that he knows something, he does not yet know as he ought to know. ³ But if anyone loves God, he is known by God.

1 CORINTHIANS 8:1-3

Take a look at verse 1 again. Paul uses two phrases that clue us in to the negative consequences of pride. The first is about knowledge, which "puffs up." The Greek word *physioo* literally means to inflate—Paul's using the word figuratively. He's getting at that feeling of pride that swells up when we know more than another person. But as we see in verse 2, that knowledge only makes us more prideful—so much so that we're blind to what we don't know.

The other phrase is "builds up." Instead of puffing up our pride and blinding us to our faults, love strengthens us. God's love is the antithesis to pride. Why? Because God's love is everything pride isn't—it's self-giving, humble, and others-focused.

Pride will make you think you're better than you really are. It will pull you away from the risk of an others-centered life. Pride can come from what we know, but it can also stem from countless other areas—our looks, our car, our job, our family, our workout routine, our house, or our church.

Pick one thing that's a source of pride for you. Maybe it's what you know about the Bible or the places you've seen in the world or the type of job you have. **Reflect on why that area of your life produces pride in you. Talk to God about it. Then spend a few minutes praying about how you could use that source of pride to serve other Christians.**

Day Four

We talked yesterday about the internal consequences of pride. Pride has a wider effect than the corruption of our hearts, though. It can cause us to harm other Christians, which is exactly what happened in Corinth.

Read 1 Corinthians 8:7–13. Some of the Corinthians evidently knew what we read yesterday—that idols aren't real gods. They took their freedom in Christ as a free ticket to dine at the pagan temples with their friends. Some people in the church thought their practices were wrong, but, since they saw their friends doing it, they felt pressured to join in.

Those who were eating meat sacrificed to idols didn't see the harm they were causing to other Christians. Paul says that to lead another Christian to act against his or her conscience is to lead them into sin.

Peek at the Greek

Paul uses the word *syneidesis*, which we translate as "conscience," three times in just seven verses. As our English translation implies, Paul's talking about the part of our brain that distinguishes between right and wrong. He repeats the word three times to emphasize his point—violating your conscience as a Christian is sin. If we think something's wrong and do it, we've sinned against God.

In their pride the Corinthians thought they, as free people in Christ, could do whatever they wanted with no consequences. But they were actually pushing people to go against their conscience, which—for those people—was sin.

This is part of the gray areas Jennie talked about in the video. There are things—such as media intake, alcohol consumption, or the price of our newest outfit—that might not trip our conscience. But it does trigger someone else's.

Think about what those gray areas might be for you. Take TV for example. What shows are you okay with watching? Does your enthusiasm for a show pressure other Christians to watch it? What could you do to consider other Christians' consciences the next time you sit down to do something with a friend?

As people who risk living an others-centered life, our goal should be to live in such a way that other Christians can look on and follow suit with a clear conscience. That might mean giving up drinking in public or buying less expensive jewelry or keeping off political Facebook threads. It might mean sacrificing for the sake of other Christians.

Day Five

In 1 Corinthians 8, we've seen another way the Corinthian church was missing the others-centered life that Jesus modeled for us. Their pride blinded them to how they were causing other Christians to sin against God. In the last verse of this chapter, Paul says he'd rather abstain from eating meat sacrificed to an idol than be the reason another Christian sinned.

The question now is how. How can we know what to abstain from in order to keep other Christians from sinning?

It begins with awareness. We can only be aware of the things that trigger other people's conscience if we know them. We have to build relationships with other Christians, especially in our local church. The friendships we develop have to go deeper than sharing a hobby or supporting the same sports team. We need to ask the deeper questions.

For example, if you're okay with drinking a beer with dinner and invite some Christian friends out for a meal, ask them what they think about drinking. Turn it into a conversation—not a debate—about what's difficult about drinking for them. Or if you're about to post a politically charged post on social media, reach out to a friend with opposing views to see if your post builds people up or actually tears them down and leads them to lash out. Listen to their point of view and take it seriously.

It all comes down to having deep, self-sacrificing relationships with other Christians. **Think about the Christians in your life right now. Pick one person whom you could talk to about what you learned in this week's study of 1 Corinthians 8. Write his or her name down. Ask if there's anything you do that could lead others—or even that person—to sin against his or her conscience. Come back to this page and write about what your friend said.**

Give Up Rights

Learning to live selflessly isn't only about setting aside our pride as we talked about last week. It's also about choosing to set aside certain rights for the good of others. Setting aside our rights paints a much broader stroke across our lives and affects more that just our eating habits.

Our lives reflect back on who Jesus is. If we want to imitate him—who gave up all of his rights as God to save us—we'll also have to make sacrifices for others. But if we don't, we show non-Christians that following Jesus doesn't really change all that much about our lives. And that simply isn't true.

At first glance, 1 Corinthians 9–10 might seem like it derails what Paul's trying to say. Keep in mind, though, that chapters 8, 9, and 10 form an entire argument about eating food sacrificed to idols. As we walk through 9 and 10 this week, we're going to discover that Paul's getting at something much deeper than what we discussed in chapter 8.

Through this session, we want to:

• Learn what it means to give up certain rights for the sake of other people.

• Feel curiosity toward how giving up rights might affect others and us.

• Identify how the rights we're exercising affect others and choose to set any aside that negatively affect Christians and non-Christians alike.

Keep those ideas in mind as we walk through the next two chapters in 1 Corinthians.

WATCH SESSION 8

THE BOOK OF 1 CORINTHIANS

WITH JENNIE ALLEN

These questions come from the free Facilitator's Guide for *The Book of 1 Corinthians* on
RightNow Media's website. If you're leading a group, download the Facilitator's Guide
to help lead discussion on Jennie's teaching and the passage from 1 Corinthians.

1   AFTER READING THE PASSAGE AND LISTENING TO JENNIE, HOW WOULD YOU
    SUMMARIZE PAUL'S MESSAGE IN THESE CHAPTERS?

2   WHAT DOES IT MEAN TO LAY DOWN OUR RIGHTS? HOW DID PAUL DO IT?
    HOW DID JENNIE DESCRIBE IT? WHAT OTHER EXAMPLES CAN YOU THINK OF?

3   WHAT DID PAUL ACCOMPLISH WHEN HE SET HIS RIGHTS ASIDE? WHAT MIGHT YOU
    HAVE TO GIVE UP SO THAT OTHER PEOPLE COULD HEAR AND BELIEVE THE GOSPEL?

4   WHAT COULD IT LOOK LIKE FOR YOU TO "SEEK THE GOOD" OF ANOTHER CHRISTIAN?

5   THIS WEEK, WHO'S ONE PERSON YOU COULD INTENTIONALLY SERVE BY SEEKING THEIR GOOD?

"

There's more joy in laying down our rights than fighting for them.

"

Day One

Jennie introduced the big idea for chapters 9 and 10 in her teaching. She said it's all about laying down our rights—about giving up the things we feel like we're owed so that other people can thrive. But what exactly does that look like?

Paul spends the first half of chapter 9 answering that question. **¹As you read 1 Corinthians 9:1–18, look for how Paul describes giving up rights. Then, look closely at 9:14–15, 18. What right does Paul have as a preacher of the gospel? What does it free him to do if he doesn't claim this right? How does it benefit the Corinthians?**

Paul could have made different decisions during life. He could have taken a wife. He could have charged money for people to hear him speak. He could have asked the Corinthian church to support him—there are biblical grounds for taking a salary while in ministry. But Paul didn't. He abdicated his rights so people could hear the gospel without being distracted by his life or financial burdens.

Re-read verse 12. ²**Why would charging people money to hear the apostles teach hinder the gospel? Who would be getting the glory if the apostles had people pay to hear them speak? Who'd get the glory if they didn't?**

Paul's concerned with exalting Jesus through his ministry. He isn't worried about where the money for his next meal will come from. He simply wants people to hear the gospel, encounter Jesus, and become disciples. If he asked people to pay to hear him preach, he'd become the main focus of his ministry instead of Jesus.

Paul's life and teaching show us we can let go of control over our lives. There's an underlying fear in all of us that says if we don't take care of ourselves, no one else will. But there's a different way—the self-giving way Jesus lived out and asks us to imitate. Paul gave up his right to control where his salary came from for the sake of God's mission and God's people. He gave up control.

---

¹⁴ *In the same way, the Lord commanded that those who proclaim the gospel should get their living by the gospel.* ¹⁵ *But I have made no use of any of these rights, nor am I writing these things to secure any such provision. For I would rather die than have anyone deprive me of my ground for boasting.* ¹⁶ *For if I preach the gospel, that gives me no ground for boasting. For necessity is laid upon me. Woe to me if I do not preach the gospel!*

1 CORINTHIANS 9:14–16

---

³**Think about one area of your life that you like to keep under your control. Maybe it's your budget or your schedule or your children. Picture what it could look like to surrender control of those things. What's one tangible step you could take today to give control over to God?**

1

2

3

Day Two

We all like to have a firm grasp on our day. We like to know what's ahead. We structure our days around our needs—what we'll eat, when we'll sleep, what we'll do at work. Without realizing it, our day can become all about us.

In our discussion about giving up our rights, it's easier to camp out on the "big" rights we can set aside for others. But how does selflessness affect our everyday lives? What does it mean to lay down our rights on a daily basis?

Open up your Bible and read 1 Corinthians 9:19–27. Paul gives several examples of how he surrenders his rights for different types of people. [1] **Looking at verse 23, what's Paul's ultimate goal in setting aside his rights?**

Paul does everything for the sake of the gospel. That means he filters every action and every thought through the goal of showing others Jesus the self-giving savior and his sacrifice that saves. Paul wants to reflect the same self-giving, sacrificial life in all he does so that people can know and follow Jesus.

So when it comes to us, we can take a step back and consider the way we approach our day. Are we ordering our days around ourselves? Or do we filter every action, every thought, around Jesus and his gospel?

Think back through your day yesterday. Consider the meals you ate, the routine you followed to get ready in the morning, the way you treated your coworkers, the attitude you had with your family, the way you acted on the road. Were you focused on yourself? On the gospel? On others?

[2] **Now think about tomorrow. Imagine what your day would be like if you filtered everything you did through showing others the gospel. What would be different about your day?**

[3] **What's one thing you could do today for another person that communicates the gospel?**

Focusing on Jesus and his gospel doesn't mean we neglect ourselves—we need to be healthy to be able to live this way. But it does mean we will put Jesus and his agenda first, which means we'll put other people before ourselves.

Commit 1 Corinthians 9:23 to memory today. Put it as your phone background or write it on a sticky note. Come back to the verse throughout the day to remind yourself to live for the sake of the gospel.

1

2

3

Day Three

Self-centered living doesn't *feel* all that bad, right? It might make us a little prideful, but at least our needs will be met and we won't have to rely on everyone else. Paul anticipates that the Corinthians might think along those lines. So at the beginning of chapter 10, he makes a case against selfish, worldly living by using a biblical example—Israel.

Read 1 Corinthians 10:1–13, and pay special attention to verses 6–7. Summarize Israel's problem in one sentence.

In every example Paul lists, Israel chose their selfish desires over God. Paul says Israel desired evil. They were idolaters. They were sexually immoral, they tested God, they complained about food. The end result of their selfish behavior was death.

Paul says Israel is an example of what *not* to do. Living selfishly leads to one thing: death. It kills us from the inside out. It poisons our relationships. It ruins our relationship with God.

But sometimes it feels like we can't help but be selfish—as if self-centeredness is our only option. But it's not. Paul doesn't want the Corinthians—or us—to throw in the towel.

² **Re-read verse 13. What does this verse say about the temptation to be selfish? What hope do we have? What encourages you about this verse in terms of choosing to be selfless?**

Paul admits that everyone will be tempted to be selfish. No one can escape it. But God has not abandoned us. With the presence of the Holy Spirit, we can withstand the temptation to be selfish. It's possible to avoid repeating Israel's history. The others-centered, selfless life of Jesus is within our grasp.

³ **Read back through verse 13 three more times out loud. Then write out a prayer asking God to help you identify when you're being tempted to be selfish and to give you the strength to choose selflessness instead. Thank him for being with you and providing a way out, even in the toughest of temptations.**

1

2

3

Day Four

Sometimes we want to pick and choose the parts of Christianity we like. Take the subject we've been talking about this week. There are some rights that are easier to give up than others. It can be tempting to keep some things under our control while being selfless only in specific areas of our lives.

But as we've already discussed in this series, following Jesus is an all-or-nothing gig. Paul wants the Corinthians to know that they can't be both selfish and selfless at the same time. It's not possible.

Read 1 Corinthians 10:14–22. When Paul talks about the cup of blessing and breaking bread, he's referencing the Lord's Supper. When we partake in the Lord's Supper—a re-creation of Jesus's final meal before he went to the cross—we remember his blood and broken body. We remember his sacrifice.

---

14 Therefore, my beloved, flee from idolatry. 15 I speak as to sensible people; judge for yourselves what I say. 16 The cup of blessing that we bless, is it not a participation in the blood of Christ? The bread that we break, is it not a participation in the body of Christ? 17 Because there is one bread, we who are many are one body, for we all partake of the one bread. 18 Consider the people of Israel: are not those who eat the sacrifices participants in the altar? 19 What do I imply then? That food offered to idols is anything, or that an idol is anything? 20 No, I imply that what pagans sacrifice they offer to demons and not to God. I do not want you to be participants with demons. 21 You cannot drink the cup of the Lord and the cup of demons. You cannot partake of the table of the Lord and the table of demons. 22 Shall we provoke the Lord to jealousy? Are we stronger than he?

1 CORINTHIANS 10:14–22

Paul says by taking the Lord's Supper, we participate in Jesus's sacrifice. In other words, the meal we take should reflect the kind of life we're living. We too should live sacrificially, just as Jesus did for us. Paul goes on to say that any type of worship that's not aimed at God is demonic. It's the complete opposite of the others-centered, selfless way of Jesus—it's selfish, indulgent, and wicked.

Re-read verse 21. The cup and table of the Lord represents the sacrificial life of Jesus and the cup and table of demons points to the exact opposite. Paul's saying the two don't go together. [1] **If you look at your life, which "table" are you sitting at? Or are you trying to sit at both?**

We can't sit at two tables in this Christian life. We have to either be fully committed to selflessly giving up our rights or not.

We can't have our cake and eat it too.

[2] **How does that idea sit with you? Take a few minutes to journal about the selfish and selfless ways of living Paul presents in this passage. What would it look like for you to be fully committed to being sacrificial, to giving up your rights? What's one right you could turn over to God for the sake of another Christian today?**

As we've said before, following Jesus means you give him our whole life. Is that something you're willing to give up?

1

2

Day Five

We've talked a lot about our rights in this session. It's not normal to give them up. But we surrender them because we follow a savior who did it first. The reasons he chose selflessness are the same for us. And that's what we'll look at today.

¹**Open up your Bible and read 1 Corinthians 10:23–33. After you've read the passage, re-read verses 24 and 31. According to these two verses, what reasons does Paul give to the Corinthians for giving up their rights?**

Paul tells the Corinthians to seek the good of their fellow Christians. In addition, everything they do should be for God's glory. That's what Jesus did. And he invites us to do the same.

We give up our rights because we follow a savior who did it first—and he did it for us. So we set aside our own agendas, our selfishness, and our pride so that other Christians and many more can follow Jesus too.

As we close out this week, think about one person in your life—maybe someone in your church or family or workplace. **What's one thing you could do to sacrifice for them?** Maybe you could give up some of your time and money to take them out to a meal, or could you sacrifice some energy to take care of their kids. Or maybe you could set aside a Saturday morning to mow their lawn.

Try it out this weekend. Then spend five minutes reflecting on what you did on the next page.

1

2

3

Worship Well Together

So far in our journey through 1 Corinthians, we've looked at a lot of the external issues in the church. They were dealing with division over leadership, sexual ethics, and food. For the first time while studying this letter, we'll peek into the Corinthians' actual worship service and see some internal problems that were also causing division.

The same self-centered attitude that caused the Corinthians to rally behind Apollos or Paul shows up in this chapter. Paul wants the church to know that selfless living isn't just something we do outside of Sunday morning. It's an all-day, everyday attitude. That means all Christians should choose to err on the side of serving other Christians, especially when it comes to how we act during corporate worship.

This chapter is one of the stickiest in 1 Corinthians. It talks about the roles of men and women—a topic widely debated in the church today. Instead of getting caught up in the debate, we'll take a step back to see Paul's big point in this chapter: How we behave in corporate worship should be others-centered, not self-centered. Keep that big idea in mind as we navigate the tough parts of 1 Corinthians 11.

Through this week's study, we want to:

- Know the ways a self-centered attitude negatively affects the church.

- Feel remorseful about our selfishness in corporate worship.

- Turn away from selfish practices that cause division and disorderliness in worship.

We hope to walk away from this session with a renewed idea about corporate worship in the church. Keep these ideas in mind as we walk through the chapter.

WATCH SESSION 9
THE BOOK OF 1 CORINTHIANS
WITH JENNIE ALLEN

These questions come from the free Facilitator's Guide for *The Book of 1 Corinthians* on RightNow Media's website. If you're leading a group, download the Facilitator's Guide to help lead discussion on Jennie's teaching and the passage from 1 Corinthians.

1　AFTER READING THE CHAPTER AND HEARING JENNIE'S TEACHING, HOW WOULD YOU DESCRIBE THE CORINTHIANS' PROBLEM WITH ORDER IN CORPORATE WORSHIP?

2　ASIDE FROM THE THINGS PAUL MENTIONS IN CHAPTER 11, WHAT ARE SOME OTHER THINGS THAT COULD POTENTIALLY DISRUPT ORDER IN A CORPORATE WORSHIP SERVICE?

3　HOW WOULD YOU DESCRIBE THE PURPOSE OF THE LORD'S SUPPER? WHAT DOES YOUR CHURCH DO TO CELEBRATE IT?

4　THINK ABOUT THE LAST TIME YOU TOOK COMMUNION AT CHURCH. WHAT WAS YOUR ATTITUDE TOWARD IT? WHAT COULD YOU DO TO REMIND YOURSELF OF THE PURPOSE OF THE LORD'S SUPPER NEXT TIME YOU TAKE IT AT CHURCH?

5　WHAT'S ONE THING YOU COULD DO TO PROMOTE ORDERLINESS IN YOUR NEXT CORPORATE WORSHIP SERVICE?

"

The Corinthians put themselves ahead of their community.

"

Day One

In Christian circles, we often say the church isn't the building—it's the people. Yes, that's true. But it doesn't mean we neglect to address how we conduct ourselves when we all meet together.

Take a moment to think about your local church service. [1]**Write down everything that happens from the moment you walk in to when you leave. What are some aspects of the service that help it flow well? How do people treat each other?**

Jennie introduced the big idea Paul hits on in 1 Corinthians 11: Members of the local church should act in an orderly, selfless way as they meet for corporate worship. As Jennie mentioned, we can make a big deal about gray-area issues—like hymnals or choir robes or altar calls—and cause division. But as we'll learn in this chapter, sometimes practices we think are normal can actually be harmful.

The local church is a big deal. It can only function properly if every member decides to be selfless. When we let selfishness get in the way, it can rip the church apart.

Read through 1 Corinthians 11:1–34. While you're reading, write down the two areas of corporate worship where the Corinthians were causing division. Also jot down any questions you might have about the passage.

We'll dive deeper into these verses in the coming days. As mentioned in the introduction, there are some tough issues in this passage. We won't be able to address everything, but we will figure out how we can choose the others-centered life in corporate worship.

Let's start this week off with prayer. Ask God to soften you to what he has to teach you through this week's study. Pray for your local church—for its leaders, staff, and volunteers. Pray God would give you a selfless attitude toward your local church as a result of studying 1 Corinthians 11.

1

2

Day Two

As we talked about yesterday, chapter 11 is all about orderliness in corporate worship. Another way to put it is, "How to live selflessly in the context of a worship service." The key is to set aside selfishness for the sake of the other people in the congregation—and that's what we'll look at today.

Read 1 Corinthians 11:1–16. **¹In your own words, how would you describe the problem Paul is addressing in these verses?**

This passage about headdresses is one of the most controversial sections in the whole Bible. We're not going to delve into the debate. But we will unpack what exactly was disrupting the orderliness of the Corinthian services.

Peek at the Greek

The word *kephalē*, which we translate as "head," is one of the most confusing and hotly debated terms in the New Testament. While there are several ways to interpret Paul's use of *kephalē*, it's important to note what he's *not* saying. Some read 1 Corinthians 11:3 as an outline of hierarchy in terms of access—the Father, Jesus, husbands, then wives. In other words, some think wives only have access to Jesus through their husbands. This idea is in direct conflict with the rest of Scripture, which says all Christians have access to God through Jesus (John 14:6; Rom 8:31–39; Eph 2:14–18; 3:10–12; 1 Tim 2:5–6; Heb 10:19–25).

Paul's concerned with how women conducted themselves in corporate worship, specifically about their headdresses. Women wore head coverings in public as a sign of modesty and respect. But when they came home, they'd take them off. Since the early church met in homes, it seems as though the women were keeping the casual, only-at-home attire during worship. Instead of dressing out of respect for the seriousness of church gathering, their clothing communicated promiscuity and disrespect.

[2] Think of it this way: Picture the most comfy outfit you'd only wear at home. Maybe it's a giant, holey T-shirt or your pajamas. Now imagine if that's all you wore to church on Sunday. Would you be distracting? What would your clothes say about you? What would they say about your attitude toward church or the people at church? After reflecting on this idea, write about what it could look like for you to be considerate of others while at church.

The problem here is less about what we wear—although that can be really important, as the example above shows—and more about our attitude. The way we dress is often motivated out of selfishness—it certainly was for the Corinthian women. A church service should be a time where Christians respect and care for each other as they worship God. If we put our personal preferences first, we'll cause problems.

Instead, we should be considerate of others. If we do, it will change the way we dress, talk, and act, especially toward other Christians.

1

2

Day Three

The church is diverse. People who follow Jesus come from all kinds of upbringings, social classes, ethnicities, countries, and cultures. The local church is also diverse—everyone comes from a different neighborhood, career, or income bracket. Our differences shouldn't create divides on Sunday morning, but they often do.

Paul cracks down on the Corinthian church in the passage we'll look at today. They're allowing social status to get in the way of their corporate worship. [1]**Read 1 Corinthians 11:17–22. Looking at verses 20–22, how would you describe the problem in the Corinthian church?**

---

[17] But in the following instructions I do not commend you, because when you come together it is not for the better but for the worse. [18] For, in the first place, when you come together as a church, I hear that there are divisions among you. And I believe it in part, [19] for there must be factions among you in order that those who are genuine among you may be recognized. [20] When you come together, it is not the Lord's supper that you eat. [21] For in eating, each one goes ahead with his own meal. One goes hungry, another gets drunk. [22] What! Do you not have houses to eat and drink in? Or do you despise the church of God and humiliate those who have nothing? What shall I say to you? Shall I commend you in this? No, I will not.

1 CORINTHIANS 11:17–22

One of the ordinances of the church is the Lord's Supper—sometimes called communion. It's the last meal Jesus ate before going to the cross and we celebrate it to remember what Jesus did for us. It's a sacred meal and it should unite Christians under Jesus's sacrifice.

Like many in the early church, Corinthians took the Lord's Supper as an invitation to eat a meal together as a congregation. But instead of going potluck-style, the Corinthians brought food only for their own families. Those who were too poor to afford a grand meal sat in the corner starving while other church members gorged themselves. Paul wanted nothing of it.

It's tempting to judge the Corinthians for their behavior. Who would ever treat another Christian that way? But the truth is, we do it too—just maybe not in the same way.

Think about your church for a moment. It can be really easy to split up into cliques at church. We hang around people in our same life stage or our same income bracket. Or, if we think back to yesterday's discussion, we choose clothing that flaunts our standard of living. We can cause the same kind of division in our church without even noticing it.

We're going to finish off today with reflection. Choose two of the following categories to journal about: income, social status, race, personal talents, children, spouse, life-stage, upbringing, career, neighborhood, hobbies. Think about each of your categories in the context of your local church. Would you say you bring unity or division when you talk about those things? What actions associated with those topics could potentially hurt someone in your church? [2]**Write out one way you'd like to be more aware of how you approach those categories.**

Worldly things like money and social standing should never divide the church. We're united through Jesus's death, burial, and resurrection. Coming together on a Sunday to worship God should bring unity—and we can choose to either contribute to or tear apart that unity.

What will it be for you?

1

2

Day Four

Have you ever experienced the feeling when everyone in the room is on the same page? Maybe it was a meeting at work when every team member got on board with a new project. Or maybe it was the thrill of a concert when the entire audience sang along. Or even when everyone in the living room cheered at a winning touchdown.

Harmony is a beautiful thing.

Yesterday we saw how the Corinthians used the Lord's Supper selfishly and caused division in the church. As we mentioned before, communion is supposed to be a time when all Christians come together—where we're all on the same page.

Read 1 Corinthians 11:23–26. After reading these verses, how would you summarize the purpose of the Lord's Supper?

The Lord's Supper has several purposes and Paul highlights three in this passage. The first is that it helps us remember what Jesus has done for us through his death. The second purpose is to proclaim Jesus's death to each other until he returns. And finally, the third is to partake of the meal together as followers of Jesus.

² **Read John 19:28–37 and consider the elements of the Lord's Supper. We have the bread and the cup. The bread symbolizes Jesus's broken body. The cup represents Jesus's spilled blood. Take a moment to write or draw about Jesus's death. How does his crucifixion affect you?**

The Lord's Supper is a sacred practice that the church has followed since it first started. The Corinthians treated it flippantly—as an intro to an indulgent, exclusive party. We can take the Lord's Supper too lightly as well. We can forget the weight of the symbolism behind the bread and cup. We can treat it like a routine. We can zone out and think about the chores for the day.

The Lord's Supper should bring us together. And that can only happen if we all take it seriously.

³ **Re-read the verses in 1 Corinthians two more times. Then think about the last time you took communion at church. What was your attitude toward it? Would you say you treated it with reverence? What would help you keep the purposes of the Lord's Supper in mind next time you take the bread and cup?**

Take a small piece of paper or a bookmark and mark 1 Corinthians 11:23–26 in your Bible. Next time you take communion, flip back to these verses. Take a few seconds to remind yourself why we take the Lord's Supper. Then pray for your church—that they'd all be on the same page.

1

2

3

Day Five

Selfishness can poison the church. We've already seen how it damaged the church in Corinth outside of their corporate worship. But this week we also realized how their selfishness ruined their worship time together.

We can fall into the same trap as the Corinthians. We can be selfish about the way we conduct ourselves in corporate worship. And it can have dire consequences. [1] **Read 1 Corinthians 11:27–34. What are the consequences that Paul names to taking the Lord's Supper in an unworthy—or selfish—way?**

God disciplines us when we're selfish about communion—or anything else involved in corporate worship. He does it to show us how seriously he takes the church. He wants the church to be unified and characterized by selfless living. That's why Paul suggests a solution to the problem at the end of the chapter. He knows God desires unity so Paul suggests a way to get there.

We can contribute to the unity of our local church too. But we have to start with us—with our attitude and conduct in corporate worship.

[2]Think about how you act during church on Sundays. Are you on your phone during the opening song? Could your clothing be distracting? Do you talk with your neighbor while your pastor preaches? Do you grumble about the worship music? What do you say about the sermon after service? Take your answers to God in prayer. Pray for forgiveness for the ways you might be acting selfishly. Ask him to show you how you can be others-focused while you're at church.

1

2

1 CORINTHIANS 12:1–14:40

Use Your Gifts

First Corinthians can feel like a beat-down. Paul isn't happy with how the church is acting, and the past eleven chapters have all been about what they need to fix. The Corinthians were selfish, which caused lots of problems. Paul's main point is that Christians should live selflessly and focus on others.

At this point in the book, we have a good idea of what *not* to do. We've looked at several ways we can put our own agendas over the needs of other Christians. Paul's given us some practical things we can do to be selfless. But in the next three chapters, Paul will explain how we can live out an others-centered life in the context of the church, specifically in terms of building up the local church in the ways God's gifted us.

In other words, Paul will show us what *to* do.

As we go through these chapters, we'll discover that the way we choose the risky life all comes down to one word—love. Loving others is the greatest risk we could ever take. But we choose to love other Christians through our gifts so that all needs are met and so that the church reflects Jesus to the world.

In this week's journey through Paul's words in 1 Corinthians 12–14, we want to:

• Know what it means to truly love other Christians in the context of the local church.

• Feel excited about the ways God could use us to build up our local church.

• Choose one way we can contribute to our local church and put it into practice.

These questions come from the free Facilitator's Guide for *The Book of 1 Corinthians* on RightNow Media's website. If you're leading a group, download the Facilitator's Guide to help lead discussion on Jennie's teaching and the passage from 1 Corinthians.

1   ACCORDING TO JENNIE'S TEACHING AND THE PASSAGE, WHAT'S THE PURPOSE BEHIND OUR GIFTS? HOW HAVE YOU SEEN SOMEONE'S GIFTS BUILD UP THE CHURCH?

2   WHAT ARE SOME OF YOUR TALENTS OR SKILLS? HOW HAS THE SPIRIT USED THEM IN YOUR LOCAL CHURCH?

3   LOOKING AT CHAPTER 13, WHAT COULD POTENTIALLY HAPPEN IF WE USED OUR GIFTS WITHOUT LOVE?

4   WHEN HAVE YOU FELT TEMPTED TO USE YOUR GIFTS FOR SELFISH REASONS? WHAT HAPPENED? WHAT DID YOU LEARN THROUGH THE PROCESS?

5   WHAT COULD YOU DO THIS WEEK TO USE THE GIFTS GOD'S GIVEN YOU TO LOVE ANOTHER PERSON IN YOUR CHURCH?

"

The truth is God shows us our gifts as we serve.

"

Day One

Before we start off today's dive into 1 Corinthians, grab your keys. If you don't have any, doodle a picture in the margin. We'll come back to them later on.

Even though there's a lot of content covered in this session, Jennie hit on the big idea that we can trace throughout all three chapters—selfless, sacrificial love. It's the same love that risks living in an others-centered way. But now we'll learn how we can individually express our love for God and his people through participation in the local church.

The Holy Spirit uses us in different ways—Paul calls it spiritual gifts. Spiritual gifts are any talents or skills you have that the Spirit works through in order to help the church. Jennie challenged us by clarifying that the gifts we have are for others, not ourselves. We use them to serve other Christians in our local church because we love them.

[1] **What are some of your talents or skills? How has the Spirit used them in your local church?**

We'll be looking at spiritual gifts a lot this week. Many churches offer spiritual gift assessments to encourage members to use their gifts in the local church. While those are great, it's important we don't lose the "why" behind using our gifts. As Jennie said, our gifts aren't for us. They're for the church. We use them to love other Christians.

Our why is love.

Look back at your key ring. For most of us, all the keys, rewards cards, and clickers are bound together on a single ring. They're united. Each item has a different function or purpose, but each is valuable and contributes to your life in some way.

That's what Paul's getting at in these chapters. We're all bound together through Jesus's love. We should therefore function as a unit. The way we act toward each other should reflect the love Jesus has given us. Because he loves us, we give his love to each other.

[2] **Use your key ring as a reminder this week. Every time you use your keys, remember Jesus's love for you. Say a short prayer of thanks when you turn on your car or unlock your front door. Ask God to use this week's study to show you one way you can express his love in your local church.**

1

2

Day Two

We have a lot of ground to cover in 1 Corinthians this week. So we're going to spend some intentional time reading all of it. Settle in for a few minutes. Put away all distractions—your phone, computer, or tablet. Take a moment to quiet your mind. If you're preoccupied with a to-do list or the stresses of your day, jot them down on a piece of scratch paper or in the margins of this book. Set it off to the side and tell yourself you'll worry about them later.

Grab your Bible and open up to 1 Corinthians 12. Read chapters 12, 13, and 14 straight through. Take your time. Let Paul's words sink in.

[1]**Write down one thing that stood out to you while you were reading. Why did that make an impression on you?**

As we heard in Jennie's teaching, all three chapters get at the same main point: Christians should faithfully contribute to the church, motivated out of love for God and for each other. In a lot of ways, chapter 13 serves as the main idea of all three chapters. It all comes down to love.

[2]**Now scan through the passage again. This time, trace the theme of love through the chapters. Write down or underline every time Paul mentions love or tells the Corinthians to act in a way that reflects love.**

We've been talking about the risk involved in the others-centered life throughout this study. Here, we find the core motivation behind taking that risk—love. When we truly love God, we'll love his people and put them before ourselves.

Love is a risk. We have to figure out if we're okay with taking that risk.

1

2

Day Three

Think about the last time you needed someone's help. Maybe you couldn't reach the top shelf at a grocery store or you asked some friends to help you move. Even though it's hard for us to admit, we all need help sometimes. The same goes for the church—we need each other.

That's Paul's point in chapter 12. He wants the church to realize that we all need each other. We can't be the church by ourselves. All of us make up Jesus's people and all of us have a purpose.

1 Read back through 1 Corinthians 12. Write down or underline every time Paul uses words like "same" or "one" or "all." Why do you think Paul uses such inclusive language?

The church operates as one unit, and Paul wants the Corinthians to see it that way. **2 Glance back over verses 4 through 7. What's the Spirit's purpose in giving us different gifts?**

The same Spirit works through each of us in unique ways. He does it for the common good of the church. The most important thing about spiritual gifts is that they are not for us. They are for everyone else for the sake of the church.

Paul lists several types of gifts in this chapter. That list isn't exhaustive or prescriptive. The Spirit can use us however he sees fit.

It's tempting to wrack our brains trying to figure out what kind of gift we have from God. But as Jennie encouraged us, it's not something to obsess over. We should be more concerned about meeting people's needs in the local church. Faithfulness to God expressed in serving his people is much more important than having a clear-cut list of gifts to pick from.

Jennie also talked about stepping in when there's a need, even when it's not in an area you're necessarily gifted. Read verse 26. When one member of the church has a problem, everyone suffers. We should be ready to spring to help out other Christians when we see them in need. And we should also be open when we need help from others.

[3] **Take a moment to journal about your local church. What's one way you could use your talents and skills in your church this week? Write out a prayer asking God to show you how to love the people in your local church.**

We're all in this church thing together. We need each other.

Which means we need you.

1

2

3

Day Four

Now that we know we have gifts from the Spirit, we need to know the proper way to use them. We don't want anything to get out of hand. We want to be selfless with our gifts. But what does that look like?

1 Corinthians 14 is another one of those sticky passages we mentioned. We aren't going to get into the issue of speaking in tongues or where women can or can't serve in the church in this study because that's not the point of this passage. As we've already seen this week, these chapters are about how to lovingly serve the church. In chapter 14, Paul's using tongues and prophecy as an example of how *not* to handle our gifts in the local church.

Take a look at verses 12 and 26. According to these verses, what's the goal of using our gifts in the church?

Peek at the Greek

Paul uses the word *oikodome*, or "building up" in English, to describe what the spiritual gifts should do for the church. *Oikodome* can also mean to increase someone or something's potential, to make more able, or to strengthen. Paul wants the Corinthians to realize that the gifts they have aren't to prop themselves up, which seems to be what's happening in their church. Instead, our gifts are to strengthen the church, to make it better and sturdier. Anything that tears down the church or causes division is outside God's intention for spiritual gifts.

No matter what gifts we have, we should always use them to build up the church. They should never be the tools we use to gain popularity or recognition. Jennie talked about it a lot in her teaching and Paul reminds us yet again in this chapter: Spiritual gifts are not about you.

[2] **Reflect on the gifts you have. Would you say you're using them for yourself or for the church?**

[3] **Close your time today in prayer. Confess to God any ways you might be using your gifts selfishly. Pray that he would give you an opportunity to be selfless with the way he's gifted you. Ask for a chance to use your gift to care for someone in your church this week.**

And when he gives you that chance, do it. Allow the Spirit to use you to build up the church.

1

2

3

Day Five

You might have noticed that we covered chapters 12 and 14, but we skipped over chapter 13. We did that on purpose. That's because we often take chapter 13 out of the context of its surrounding chapters. We read it at weddings or during a marriage series, which can make us think chapter 13 is all about romantic love.

But that's not really what it's about.

As we've explored these three chapters this week, we've seen that the love described in 1 Corinthians 13 is actually about how we treat other Christians in the context of the local church. It's the sacrificial, selfless love of Jesus.

We've already put some spiritual disciplines into practice during this study. This week, we're going to try one called Lectio Divina, which is just a fancy Latin way of saying "prayerful reading."

We're going to take you through the four steps of Lectio Divina, which will help you pray and think deeply about 1 Corinthians 13. While you go through this exercise, remember the message of chapters 12 and 14. How does this description of love help us better understand those two chapters?

Take your time for each step. This isn't something to rush through, so make sure you have plenty of time before you start.

Lectio (Read): Remove all distractions and quiet your mind before God. Now read 1 Corinthians 13 three times slowly. If you can, read it out loud to yourself. Let the message hit you. After reading it three times, find one verse or phrase that stands out to you the most. Re-read it a couple more times and place emphasis on different words as you read.

Meditatio (Meditate): Think about the phrase or verse that stood out to you. What does it mean? What does it say about God? Humans? How does it contribute to the big idea we've talked about in 1 Corinthians?

Oratio (Pray): Pray through your verse or phrase. Ask God to show you what he's saying through this verse. Take your verse and turn it into a prayer. For example, if you chose verse 4, you could pray, "Teach me to be patient and kind," or, "Thank you for being patient and kind with me."

Contemplatio (Contemplate): Now that you've read, thought, and prayed through the text, finish off your time in silence. Ask God to speak to you. Pray he'd show you one practical thing you could apply to your life from this passage. Then listen. Write down what he says and then do it.

If I speak in the tongues of men and of angels, but have not love, I am a noisy gong or a clanging cymbal. [2] And if I have prophetic powers, and understand all mysteries and all knowledge, and if I have all faith, so as to remove mountains, but have not love, I am nothing. [3] If I give away all I have, and if I deliver up my body to be burned, but have not love, I gain nothing.

[4] Love is patient and kind; love does not envy or boast; it is not arrogant [5] or rude. It does not insist on its own way; it is not irritable or resentful; [6] it does not rejoice at wrongdoing, but rejoices with the truth. [7] Love bears all things, believes all things, hopes all things, endures all things.

[8] Love never ends. As for prophecies, they will pass away; as for tongues, they will cease; as for knowledge, it will pass away. [9] For we know in part and we prophesy in part, [10] but when the perfect comes, the partial will pass away. [11] When I was a child, I spoke like a child, I thought like a child, I reasoned like a child. When I became a man, I gave up childish ways. [12] For now we see in a mirror dimly, but then face to face. Now I know in part; then I shall know fully, even as I have been fully known.

[13] So now faith, hope, and love abide, these three; but the greatest of these is love.

1 CORINTHIANS 13

★ **LECTIO DIVINA**

Lectio Divina (Latin for "Divine Reading") dates back to the prayerful reading of the early church fathers. The four-step discipline was formalized by the twelfth century. This practice focuses on treating the Bible as God's living Word and includes four separate parts. It begins with reading, then moves to reflection, prayer, and contemplation. The goal of Lectio Divina is to commune with God by interacting with his Word and listening to the Spirit.

Hope In The Resurrection

Paul has been encouraging the church in Corinth to take the risk of living an others-centered life. This way of living exhibits the sacrificial love of Jesus in all areas of life from the local church to the family to the workplace. We live selflessly only through the power of the Holy Spirit, fueled by the self-giving love of Jesus.

As Paul brings his letter to a close, he'll point to the biggest reason for choosing selflessness. It's the most important part of the gospel—without it we'd have no good news.

First Corinthians 15 is all about Jesus's resurrection. Since Jesus rose from the dead, we have life and hope and salvation. If he were still dead, the gospel wouldn't exist. The message would be that a man with interesting abilities died at the hands of the Romans. The end.

But he's not dead. He's alive. And that's a big deal not just for today, but also for all eternity.

The resurrection is the reason we choose the risky life today and it's the foundation of our hope in what will come when Jesus returns.

As we study the future resurrection this week, we want to:

• Understand the significance of the resurrection in our lives today and in what will come in eternity.

• Feel joyful about the fact that we will be raised from the dead.

• Choose the risky, others-centered life daily knowing that living this way is not in vain.

The resurrection changes everything. We'll see just how important it is to our lives throughout this week.

WATCH SESSION 11
THE BOOK OF 1 CORINTHIANS
WITH JENNIE ALLEN

★ QUESTIONS FOR SMALL GROUP DISCUSSION

These questions come from the free Facilitator's Guide for *The Book of 1 Corinthians* on RightNow Media's website. If you're leading a group, download the Facilitator's Guide to help lead discussion on Jennie's teaching and the passage from 1 Corinthians.

1   WHAT'S YOUR UNDERSTANDING OF JESUS'S RESURRECTION? HAVE YOU THOUGHT OF IT AS A BIG DEAL? OR IS IT SOMETHING YOU DON'T THINK A LOT ABOUT?

2   ACCORDING TO THE PASSAGE AND JENNIE'S TEACHING, WHY IS JESUS'S RESURRECTION IMPORTANT? HOW DOES IT RELATE TO OUR FUTURE RESURRECTION?

3   WHAT'S YOUR VISION OF ETERNITY? WHAT QUESTIONS DO YOU HAVE?

4   WHAT DO YOU THINK IT MEANS FOR US AS JESUS'S FOLLOWERS, WHO ANTICIPATE THE RESURRECTION, TO LIVE WELL TODAY WHILE ALSO HOPING FOR WHAT WILL HAPPEN WHEN JESUS RETURNS?

5   WHAT COULD YOU DO THIS WEEK TO REMIND YOURSELF OF THE HOPE WE HAVE IN ETERNITY WITH GOD?

"

Death will not have the final word.

"

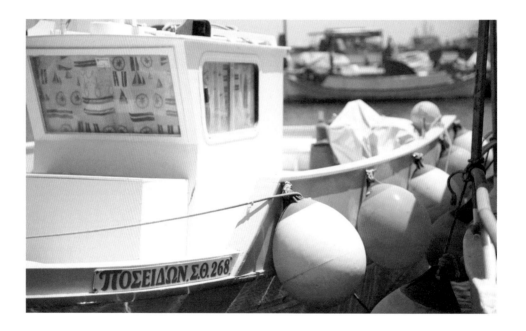

Day One

Have you ever wondered why we call the gospel "good news"? We often answer that question by talking about how Jesus has saved us from hell or that he died on the cross for our sins. It's all true. But those aspects on their own aren't what make the gospel good.

The gospel is good news because Jesus is alive. If he were still in that grave, we'd have nothing to be excited about. Nothing. We'd still be as dead in our sin as his body would be in the tomb.

But he is not dead. He is risen.

Jennie called Jesus's resurrection the linchpin of our faith. Without that resurrection, we have no hope, no purpose, no life. Everything hinges on the fact that Jesus defeated death. If he's alive—and he is—we know that death on this earth is not the end of the story. We will be raised too.

[1] In a few sentences, summarize your understanding of Jesus's resurrection. Have you thought of it as a big deal? Or is it something you don't think a lot about?

We often forget—or neglect—the resurrection in our everyday lives. But it's the very reason we're able to be followers of Jesus. It changes everything. This week, we're going to unpack the resurrection and see why it's a big deal.

[2] Open up your Bible and read all of 1 Corinthians 15. When you're done, write out a short prayer thanking God for Jesus's resurrection and our future resurrection. Ask him to use this week's study to deepen your understanding of the resurrection.

1

2

Day Two

Sometimes it's good to get back to the basics. In the final chapters of 1 Corinthians, Paul draws the church back to its roots. He reminds them of what he first taught them when he visited their city years before. It all comes back to the gospel.

[1] **Read 1 Corinthians 15:1–8. Summarize Paul's explanation of the gospel in your own words. What idea is at the center of the gospel according to Paul?**

The resurrection is the foundation of our faith. Paul wants the Corinthians to remember that truth. He goes out of his way to prove it's true by bringing up all the people who saw Jesus after he rose from the dead. Hundreds of men and women witnessed him. In other words, believing in the resurrection isn't foolish—it's the very thing we stand upon as Christians.

Jesus's resurrection, though, isn't the only thing we buy into when we say he's alive. Since he's risen, it means we too will be raised to new life. It also means that even though we might die before Jesus returns, that's not the end of our story. We will rise to meet new life one day.

But for some reason, many people in the Corinthian church didn't believe Christians would rise again. Open your Bible and read 1 Corinthians 15:12–19. [2] **What consequences does Paul list that come with denying the resurrection of Christians?**

If we deny that Jesus will one day return and resurrect Christians who've died, we essentially deny that Jesus is alive. His resurrection points to our future. If it didn't happen, then when we die, we just die. We make God and the witnesses of Jesus's resurrection liars. And we have no hope.

That's why Paul drives home his point about the resurrection to the Corinthians. They believe Jesus is alive—if they didn't, they wouldn't be Christians. That means they must believe they will live again when Jesus returns. It's a non-negotiable.

All our hope rests on the fact that when we die, we're simply closing our eyes on the temporary and will open them to the eternal.

[3] **Spend some time journaling about the resurrection, specifically about the future resurrection when Jesus returns. Since death on this earth isn't the end of our story, how does the resurrection shape the way you think about dying? What fears do you have? What questions?**

1

2

3

Day Three

We've talked a lot about the risky, others-centered life in this study of 1 Corinthians. Living this way is a risk because we put our own security, well-being, and control of our lives aside so that we can meet the needs of other Christians. We give ourselves away because we love Jesus and his love for us compels us to act like him.

But there's another reason we choose to live focused on others. Paul points it out in 1 Corinthians 15. Open up your Bible and read 1 Corinthians 15:29–34.

★ CONSIDER THIS

We've come across yet another sticky passage in 1 Corinthians. At first glance, verse 29 seems to imply that you can be baptized on behalf of someone else to help them get saved. However, this is the only time in the Bible anything close to that idea is ever mentioned. The better explanation is that Paul's talking about the symbolism behind baptism of being buried and raised to life. Paul's saying if we don't believe in the resurrection, it doesn't make sense to use baptism as a symbol of resurrection.

Paul uses his own life as an example of the risk of living focused on others. His life is always in danger. Why would he put himself through all that turmoil for no good reason? He wants the Corinthians to see that, since Christians will be resurrected from the dead, we can live in obedience to God today and know that it's not in vain.

In verse 32, Paul implies that if there's no resurrection, we should be able to do whatever we want. **In your own words, why would the resurrection give you a reason to avoid giving in to the temptation to do whatever you want?**

While it's tempting to take advantage of this life and live it to the fullest, that's not what Jesus has called us to. He's asked us to live like he did. He sacrificed for other people. He obeyed and did whatever the Father told him to do. He gave up his rights for our sake.

We're following in the footsteps of our risen king. He defeated death. He will return and raise us to life.

We live the risky, others-centered life because of what Jesus has done. We live it because we know what's to come. We know it's worth it.

Because he said so. And he's proven it to be true by walking out of that tomb.

But the question still remains: Will you choose the risky life?

1

Day Four

One danger we face when we think about the future—Jesus's return and our resurrection—is that we can get caught up in the details. We can fret about the specifics of when it will happen or how it will happen or what kind of bodies we'll have. Paul cautions us against that type of thinking because we cannot fully know what will happen until it actually happens. But he does offer some answers, and that's what we'll unpack today.

Read 1 Corinthians 15:35–44. **List the words Paul uses to describe our resurrected bodies.**

When we think about the resurrection of our bodies when Jesus returns, we sometimes picture some sort of translucent, ghost-like body that floats around with a harp in hand. But that's not at all what Paul's describing in this passage. He uses words like "imperishable," "power," and "spiritual."

Peek at the Greek

Paul describes our resurrected bodies as spiritual, or *pneumatikos*. While *pneumatikos* often refers to something being the opposite of physical—spirit, intangible, immaterial—we shouldn't jump to the idea that our resurrected bodies will not be physical. Rather, Paul uses this word to talk about the difference between our fallen, earthly bodies and our renewed, sinless bodies that we'll carry into eternity. Those very physical bodies will be free from sin and death entirely.

We will have real, tangible, physical bodies. Just look at the accounts of Jesus's resurrection for proof. He ate and walked. His disciples touched his hands and side. His resurrection body points to the kind of body we'll have in eternity.

² **Reflect on the negative impact sin has on the body you have now. You get sick. You can lose control of your emotions. You can be mentally traumatized. Now, think about what you would feel in a body that never experienced those things. What gets you most excited about having that kind of body in the future?**

The physical resurrection of our bodies will come. We have so much hope. And the best part about that hope is that it's anchored in the promise of God and the resurrection of Jesus.

1

2

Day Five

People often spend their lives trying to avoid death. Our culture obsesses over youth. No one wants to grow old. No one wants to appear weak. No one wants to die. We'll do anything to keep us from meeting the end of our lives. And when the end comes, we don't know what to do.

1 Imagine you woke up tomorrow to discover you had a superpower—you can never die. How would your life be different? What would you change about the way you live?

Immortality isn't far-fetched for us as Christians. Death on this earth is just the beginning of the story for us. We don't have to fear death because Jesus already defeated it. Read 1 Corinthians 15:51–57.

---

51 *Behold! I tell you a mystery. We shall not all sleep, but we shall all be changed,* 52 *in a moment, in the twinkling of an eye, at the last trumpet. For the trumpet will sound, and the dead will be raised imperishable, and we shall be changed.* 53 *For this perishable body must put on the imperishable, and this mortal body must put on immortality.* 54 *When the perishable puts on the imperishable, and the mortal puts on immortality, then shall come to pass the saying that is written:*

"Death is swallowed up in victory."

55 *"O death, where is your victory?*

O death, where is your sting?"

56 *The sting of death is sin, and the power of sin is the law.* 57 *But thanks be to God, who gives us the victory through our Lord Jesus Christ.* 58 *Therefore, my beloved brothers, be steadfast, immovable, always abounding in the work of the Lord, knowing that in the Lord your labor is not in vain.*

1 CORINTHIANS 15:51–58

Paul gives us yet another picture of what will come when Jesus returns. We will experience immortality. We will be changed. Death will be defeated once and for all.

Our lives on earth will pass by like a breath. But we live today for what will last.

[2] **Read 1 Corinthians 15:58. What does this verse say about what we do during this life? How does that truth shape your attitude toward your job? Family? Friends? Church?**

With the promises of eternity in our minds and the work of Jesus as our foundation, we can persevere through anything in this life. Any pain or sorrow we experience can point us back to Jesus who endured the same. It can also point us forward to the resurrection we will experience because he rose from the dead first.

[3] **Spend some time reflecting on the truths from this week's study. Try reading back through 1 Corinthians 15 slowly—or even out loud—allowing the Spirit to solidify the message in your mind and heart. Write down a prayer of gratitude to God for what he has already done for you through Jesus, what he's doing in you now, and what he will do when Jesus returns.**

1

2

3

Take The Risk

We've made it. We're in the final chapter of 1 Corinthians. We've followed Paul's words to the fledgling church in Corinth. He's had to correct a lot of self-centered behavior. He's advocated for a risky, others-centered life that chooses sacrifice over selfishness, service over self-advancement.

It's been a tough journey. Paul hasn't left many stones unturned. He's addressed every issue in the church from sexual immorality to leadership battles to food choice. While much of 1 Corinthians feels like a drag through the mud, Paul isn't going to leave the Corinthians there. He ends with a strong glimmer of hope.

Chapter 16 shows how living selflessly affects a wide variety of people. When we put other Christians first, it inspires them to do the same—and that's exactly what we see in this chapter. The people Paul has invested in are now giving themselves for Jesus, his mission, and his people. Paul invites the Corinthians—and us—to do the same.

In this final session, we want to:

• Know that, when we focus on others, it has a large impact, inspiring other Christians to do the same.

• Feel excited about taking the next step into the risky life.

• Identify and take one step of obedience toward the others-centered life.

As always, keep those goals in mind as we journey through this final session of 1 Corinthians.

WATCH SESSION 12
THE BOOK OF 1 CORINTHIANS
WITH JENNIE ALLEN

★ QUESTIONS FOR SMALL GROUP DISCUSSION

These questions come from the free Facilitator's Guide for *The Book of 1 Corinthians* on
RightNow Media's website. If you're leading a group, download the Facilitator's Guide
to help lead discussion on Jennie's teaching and the passage from 1 Corinthians.

1   NOW THAT WE'VE MADE IT THROUGH THE WHOLE BOOK, HOW WOULD YOU SUMMARIZE
    PAUL'S PURPOSE AND MESSAGE BEHIND THIS LETTER?

2   IN THIS FINAL CHAPTER, WHAT DOES PAUL DO AND SAY TO SHOW HIS LOVE TO THE CORINTHIANS
    AND OTHER CHRISTIANS?

3   WHY DO YOU THINK PAUL ENCOURAGED THE CORINTHIANS TO DO EVERYTHING IN LOVE?
    WHAT COULD IT LOOK LIKE TO LOVE PEOPLE IN THE SAME WAY PAUL DID?

4   WHAT'S ONE THING GOD'S TAUGHT YOU THROUGH THIS STUDY OF 1 CORINTHIANS?
    WHAT COULD YOU DO TO APPLY WHAT YOU'VE LEARNED TO YOUR LIFE THIS WEEK?

"

Don't get distracted. Be steadfast. Stand firm.

"

Day One

Jennie pointed to the hope we find in 1 Corinthians 16. Though this letter has been full of criticism and harsh rebuke, there's still a way forward. The Corinthians aren't stuck. They can turn away from selfishness and toward the risky life Paul's talked about throughout his letter.

And the same is true for us.

We aren't stuck. We have a way forward.

1 Settle in for a few minutes and read through 1 Corinthians 16. Then in your own words, write a couple sentences summarizing how this chapter ends the book on a hopeful note.

While the ending of 1 Corinthians might seem like a simple list of names and greetings, Paul's words point to a deep truth about what it means to live the others-centered life. By greeting people and advising the Corinthians to do the same, Paul shows the impact the risky life can have on other people.

Living selflessly means we give up our finances for other people. It means we organize our time around serving other Christians. It means extending hospitality to Christians. It ultimately unifies us. It causes us to stand firm. It brings growth to the whole church.

Jennie spoke about how important it is to put other people first. Paul always looked to the people he ministered to instead of himself. We can do the same.

[2] **As we move forward into our last week in 1 Corinthians, spend some time talking to God. Write out a short prayer asking God to show you how you can invest in one other believer you know. Pray for that person by name. Write it down. Pray for him or her throughout your day and pray the Spirit would show you one way to love that person this week.**

1

2

Day Two

The others-centered life can be easier to define within our immediate circle. We can think of specific Christians, like we did yesterday, and intentionally invest in them. As we've seen throughout 1 Corinthians, however, the risky life shouldn't be confined to our circle of Christian friends. It applies to our entire lives. It applies to the entire church.

¹Take a look at 1 Corinthians 16:1–4. In a sentence or two, summarize what Paul's asking the Corinthian church to do.

All of Paul's church plants were collecting funds for the church in Jerusalem. While the money was partially for the impoverished members of the church there, it also had a symbolic purpose.

The early church suffered from tension between Jewish and Gentile (non-Jewish) believers. It took many debates and eyewitness accounts to convince the Jewish Christians in Jerusalem that the Gentiles also fully believed in Jesus. The apostles had already affirmed Gentile Christians, but the two groups still had trouble unifying.

So Paul decided to prompt his primarily Gentile-populated churches to ease the tension. That's why he asks the Corinthians to collect an offering for the church in Jerusalem. He's asking them to put the Jewish believers first—to put unity first.

We're back to the risk involved in an others-centered life. It has the potential to affect all Christians—especially those we don't necessarily get along with.

Pull out your phone or computer for a moment. Find the list of your friends or followers on your most-used social media site—or open your contacts on your phone or email. Scroll through the list of names for a minute. Of the Christians on your list, who would you struggle to give money to? Why? Spend some time journaling about your attitude toward those people.

What could it look like to be so others-centered that you put your own feelings aside to serve another Christian?

It's something only you can answer. Will you dare to take the risk?

1

2

Day Three

If you had one last thing to say to your family and friends, what would you say? What would you want them to know? That's where we find Paul in this section of 1 Corinthians. He's in the last paragraphs of his letter. He has one last shot to drive his message home.

Paul closes by addressing people by name and giving the Corinthians some specific instructions. Go back through 1 Corinthians 16:5–24. **¹Of the people Paul mentions, who stands out to you? Why?**

Paul's final words point back to the big idea we've talked about in 1 Corinthians. As Christians, we should put other believers before ourselves. Paul has been doing it all along—he's traveled and preached so others could become Christians and grow as disciples.

He wants the Corinthians to act in the same way. He admonishes them to have the courage to put other believers first and to do it all in love.

Peek at the Greek

In 1 Corinthians 16:13, the ESV and NASB translate the word *andrizomai* as "act like men," but most other translations say "be courageous" or "show courage." As Jennie mentioned in the video, *andrizomai* is a military term to describe the courage a soldier has in the face of danger. Rather than making a statement about masculinity, Paul uses *andrizomai* to show the seriousness of persistence in the Christian life. In fact, all of the words Paul uses in this verse have military connotations, as if he's calling the Corinthians to see their Christian lives as warfare. But Paul accents his call to military-like vigor with a command to do all things in love in verse 14.

[2] More than any other passage we've read, this chapter reminds us that 1 Corinthians is a letter. Paul wrote to specific people who would have read the entire letter in one sitting. Even though we have a little left to cover in 1 Corinthians, carve out some time this week to read the entire letter in one go. Afterwards, take a moment to reflect on your experience. What did you notice in that reading that you hadn't so far in our study? What did you discover about the character of God?

1

2

Day Four

We've talked a lot about the risky life that puts other people before us. It's a risk because it means we might have to live with un-met needs. We might have sacrifice time, energy, or money. We might have to say no to something we want for the sake of another Christian.

But why? Why should we choose to live in such a crazy, counter-cultural way? Paul continues to remind us throughout 1 Corinthians of why we put other people first. And he brings it up again in this final chapter.

Read 1 Corinthians 16:14 five times slowly, letting the words sink in. [1]**Why do you think Paul encouraged the Corinthians to do everything in love?**

The others-centered way of living comes down to love. We keep coming back to that word because it's the foundation of the risky life Jesus modeled for us and invites us to apply to our lives.

Jesus gave up his rights. He chose pain when he could have avoided it. He decided to shake hands with death.

Because he loves us.

Now he asks us to show that same love.

Paul encourages the Corinthians to do everything in love. Everything. That means we fold our laundry, drive to work, and sing on Sunday morning with love. It means we forgive the back-stabbing friend and withhold from posting harsh words on social media. It means we love. No matter the cost.

[2]Make a list of everything you do in a day. Be as detailed as you want. Pick one of those things and brainstorm what it could look like to walk through that part of your day with Jesus's sacrificial love. Then, try it out. Ask the Spirit to help you love as Jesus did.

[3]Come back to this page and reflect on your experience. What did you learn? How did your actions affect other people? Yourself?

Then do it again the next day.

1

2

3

Day Five

We're at the end of our study and it's time to make a choice. We've asked this question for the past twelve weeks, and now it's up to you to answer.

Will you choose this risky, others-centered life?

[1]**After all we've discussed about the others-centered life, how would you define it for yourself?**

The selfless life is unglamorous. It requires you to give up what you value the most—your time, your energy, your money, your talents, your personal preferences. It asks you to say no to yourself and yes to other Christians. It means putting yourself on the line so that your brothers and sisters can thrive.

But choosing that life is worth it.

Because when Christians put each other first, something miraculous happens. Everyone's needs are met. The risk pays off.

Picture your life as it stands today. Think about all the needs and worries that flood your day. Now imagine if the Christians around you met every single one of those needs without being prompted—just because they love you. How would your life be different?

That's the kind of life God envisions for his people. He wants us to look out for each other, to risk it all for each other. It's simple to say, but not so easy to live out.

If that kind of life isn't happening now in your church, that means someone has to take the first step. Someone has to decide to take the risk on other Christians. Someone has to meet other believers' needs first.

That's where you come in.

[2] **Spend some time in prayer asking God what he wants you to do next. Pray for one specific step you can take this week to be others-centered, to take a risk. Write down your one risky step.**

And then do it.

1

2

Members of the RightNow team involved in creating this video Bible study and study guide include:

Brian Mosley: President
Phil Warner: VP, Video Production
Paul Lanum: VP, Publishing & Conferences
Matt Wood: VP, Marketing
Jackie Mosley: Sr. Publisher
Chad Madden: Sr. Producer, Cinematography, Video Editor, Motion Graphics, Colorist
Mark Blitch: Video Editor
Courtney Davis: Field Producer, Video Editor
Brendon Lankford: Cinematography
Cameron Rhodes: Cinematography, Video Editor
Jed Ostoich: Associate Publisher
Sophie DeMuth: Writer
Mike Marshall: Creative Director
Mateo Boyd: Graphic Designer

Video Team Contributors: Lindsie Herring, Josh Holden, Will Irwin, Jason Jean, Clint Loveness, Lindsey McNally, Lee Sherman, Madi Simpson, Bradley Van Strien, Mark Weaver

Publishing Team Contributors: Alyssa Gossom, Collin Huber, Kelley Mathews

Design Team Contributors: Charles Dew, Megan Kvalvik, Daniel Lu, Jeff Smith

THE BOOK OF
1ST CORINTHIANS